LIVE LEAD LEARN

Gail Kelly holds a number of international roles: member of the Group of Thirty, the Global Board of Advisors to the US Council on Foreign Relations, member of the McKinsey Advisory Council, senior global adviser to UBS and director of Woolworths Holdings in South Africa. Within Australia, she is a director of Country Road Group, David Jones and Australian Philanthropic Services. In addition, she is an adjunct professor at the University of New South Wales, and ambassador for women's empowerment for CARE Australia. Gail retired as CEO of the Westpac Group in February 2015, which marked the culmination of her 35-year career in banking. She is married to Allan and they have four children.

GAIL KELLY

LIVE LEAD LEARN

My stories of life and leadership

VIKING

an imprint of

PENGUIN BOOKS

VIKING

UK | USA | Canada | Ireland | Australia
India | New Zealand | South Africa | China

Penguin Books is part of the Penguin Random House group of companies
whose addresses can be found at global.penguinrandomhouse.com.

Penguin
Random House
Australia

First published by Penguin Random House Australia Pty Ltd, 2017

1 3 5 7 9 10 8 6 4 2

Text copyright © Gail Kelly 2017.

The moral right of the author has been asserted.

Cover design by Alex Ross © Penguin Random House Australia Pty Ltd
Text design by Samantha Jayaweera © Penguin Random House Australia Pty Ltd
Cover photography by Tim Bauer
Typeset in 12/16pt Adobe Garamond by Samantha Jayaweera,
Penguin Random House Australia Pty Ltd
Colour separation by Splitting Image Colour Studio, Clayton, Victoria
Printed and bound in Australia by Griffin Press, an accredited ISO AS/NZS
14001 Environmental Management Systems printer.

National Library of Australia
Cataloguing-in-Publication data:

Kelly, Gail.
Live, lead, learn : my stories of life and leadership / Gail Kelly.
9780670079391 (paperback)
Subjects: Kelly, Gail.
Businesswomen--Australia.
Leadership in women--Australia.
Bank directors--Australia.
Women directors of corporations--Australia.
Corporate governance--Australia.
Work-life balance.

ISBN 9780670079391

penguin.com.au

To the five most important people in my life:
Allan, Sharon, Sean, Mark and Annie

CONTENTS

Author's Note

'There is no passion to be found playing small – in settling for a life that is less than the one you are capable of living.'

This is something that Nelson Mandela is thought to have said. I like the quote. Don't play small. Good is not good enough. Follow your passion. Back yourself. Be yourself. Love what you do. You are capable of way more than you think you are.

I believe this. It is my experience.

I am the first to acknowledge that my life journey has been an improbable one. Latin teacher to banker. Teller to major-bank CEO. Pretoria girl to board member of the Business Council of Australia. Member of the Group of Thirty and a global adviser to the US Council on Foreign Relations. Wife and mother of four – including triplets.

I am also the first to acknowledge that I have had a lot of luck. And along the way, I've learned an enormous amount. In this book, I share what I have learned, my insights and experiences on what it takes to live a happy life and to be successful in leadership. This is not a memoir or a self-help book. It is not an academic textbook. To the contrary, it is intensely practical. I use my own stories and experience, personal and business, to bring the lessons and key themes to life.

My hope is that this book will help others – from all ages, all stages in their careers, across a range of different industries. Perhaps lessons I have gleaned in life and leadership will trigger some thoughts of things to try, things to change, priorities to reset. Please let me know if it does.

Introduction

On the weekend of 17–19 October 2008, five weeks after the fall of Lehman Brothers, a small group of banking chief executive officers from around the world gathered in an old-world hotel perched on a mountainside near Florence. Representing Westpac, I was the CEO from Australia. My colleagues came from a wide range of banks, including Citibank, Goldman Sachs, the Bank of New York Mellon, Standard Chartered, UniCredit, Sberbank and Sumitomo Mitsui. Larry Summers, a former US secretary of treasury, had joined the group as guest speaker. The management consultancy group McKinsey & Co. was our host.

The meeting had a surreal feel to it. There was an acute understanding that the global financial system was in crisis. Equity markets had plummeted. Credit markets were in lockdown. The fear and panic that had gripped Wall Street on the day Lehman Brothers filed for bankruptcy had sent shockwaves around the world. Unlike Bear Stearns earlier in the year, Lehman Brothers had been allowed to fail. There was to be no bailout. The contagion spread fast, and each day brought fresh news of financial institutions in difficulty. Central bankers globally were linking arms and moving at pace, injecting billions into the financial system. Governments too were mobilising, developing coordinated responses. The previous weekend, the G20 finance ministers and the International Monetary Fund had met in Washington to put together a plan to best support the global economy.

In our small conference room, the mood was sombre. CEOs spoke candidly and thoughtfully as each of us shared our experience of the past six months. Some of the CEOs had been personally involved over that dramatic weekend of 12–14 September in the attempts to find a lifeline for Lehman Brothers. How had we got to this point? Why had the US government responded in one way to the Bear Stearns crisis and in another to Lehman Brothers? Who might be next? What were the likely implications for financial institutions and their business models for the future? For economies around the world, for industries, for jobs, for people, the consequences of this financial crisis might prove to be devastating. For two days, we listened and we talked. I had a sense of being enclosed in a calm and centred space while giant forces of change were erupting outside.

In 48 hours, I would be back in Sydney and back at my desk. I had a lot to think about. Eight months into my new job, my agenda encompassed considerable complexity and challenge. While Australia had already been significantly impacted by the evolving financial crisis, the Lehman Brothers collapse intensified the pressure. It was clear that the real economy was going to be damaged, that businesses and people would suffer. As Westpac CEO, my first priority was to steer the company through the crisis. It was not, however, my only imperative. Our merger with Australia's fifth-largest bank, St.George Bank, was weeks away from being finalised. It was critical that this transaction be successful and that we deliver on its promise. I was also deeply mindful of the ambitious mandate given to me by the board at the time of my appointment. 'Transform the Westpac Group around customers' – this was my charge.

As I packed my bags and headed for home, I asked myself the question: do I have what it takes to do this?

I realised that I would need to draw on every life and leadership lesson of my journey so far. I would need to dig deep and back myself. It would be essential to keep learning. Little did I know that some of my biggest lessons on how to live and lead were yet to come.

PART I

FOUNDATIONS

Life lessons learned early

I

A LUCKY
START

Women are quick to call out luck and support from others when talking of their leadership success. Men are more upfront about their own talents and skills. This is my experience. The truth is, of course, be you male or female, achieving leadership success requires the combination of a lot of things: hard work, intellect, skills, personal support, a great team, courage, determination, luck. Luck is always in the mix. It could be pure luck, the sort of random luck of where or when you were born, of the genes you inherited; it could be being in the right place at the right time sort of luck; it could be the 'make it happen' luck that comes from practising hard, from being prepared to put yourself out there and have a go. My story has all these elements. I am particularly cognisant of its lucky start. My parents, the choices they made, their love for my brother and I – we had the very best of foundations.

There is some commonality in the backgrounds of my parents, Herby and Pat Currer. Both came from large working-class families with roots in England and Scotland. Both were born in South Africa, 11 months apart, with my father the youngest of four sons and my mother the youngest of four daughters. The 1929 depression hit the families hard, and neither of my parents finished school. There was, in addition, something about each of them that set them apart – a fighting spirit, a drive and determination to make something of themselves and of life, and a willingness to work hard.

For my father these qualities came to the fore early, and they came accompanied with a remarkable natural sporting ability. His was the type of skill that made everything to do with a ball seem really easy. As it happened, it was football that became his passion. Together with two of his older brothers, Herby played for Arcadia Football Club in Pretoria in the championship-winning seasons of the early 1930s. In 1933, at the age of 16, he was selected to represent South Africa, and was called out as being the youngest ever footballer to win Springbok colours. Encouraged by his father, William Currer, he decided to pursue a professional football career and in 1936 he headed to Scotland to play for the Aberdeen Football Club. A Pretoria newspaper reported:

It was feared by many that when overseas teams saw Currer
in action he would be enticed away from us, and the inevitable
has happened.

Sadly for my father, serious ligament damage to his knee cut
short his professional career, and in early 1940, after the onset of
the Second World War, he returned to South Africa. His journey
was an exciting one as soon after departing, his ship, the Dunbar
Castle, hit a German mine in the English Channel. My father loved
to tell the story, and he told it vividly. He spoke of being woken up
by the explosion and, dressed only in his pyjamas, rushing to the
deck and helping women and children into lifeboats. He described
what it felt like to be rowing through the choppy, icy waters, then
looking back and seeing the sinking ship. As children, we were riveted. To us, he was a hero.

Once back in South Africa, he sought out his first sweetheart,
the young woman from Durban whom he had left behind four
years earlier. Herby was not sure how this would go. While in
Aberdeen, he had been a very poor correspondent and after a year
or so, had stopped writing altogether. For her part, she was both
too proud and too much of a realist to wait around. Fortunately
the flame between them rekindled quickly, and within a matter of
months the young couple was married.

Vibrant, spirited, intelligent, with a love for life: these are words
that capture the essence of my mother Patricia – or Pat, as she liked to
be called. She hated housework and as the youngest of the Pettigrew
girls, and adored by her mother and sisters, she was largely let off
domestic chores. Her two major passions were her animals and her
books. Dogs, cats, birds, ducks, geese, even monkeys, at various

times she had them all. She also brought a healing touch and a great deal of care to any in the neighbourhood that were sick, neglected or hurt. As for reading, she loved it. For a period the family lived in a house belonging to a Jewish family. In the outside shed my mother discovered piles of books, many of them on Jewish history and tradition. She delighted in the beauty and richness of language and was captivated by the stories. Her greatest sadness was the premature ending of her schooling. A severe bout of scarlet fever led to six weeks in a hospital isolation ward and a bleak period of recuperation. That was it for her in terms of formal education. Her father determined that his youngest daughter had had enough, and that, in any event, finishing school was not necessary for a girl. Mum was soon bored at home and decided to take a course in shorthand and typing. Her first job was with a firm of solicitors, McKintosh and Cross, earning £7 a month. She loved the independence.

While Pat and Herby married in their early twenties, a full 13 years passed before my brother, Trevor, was born. His surprise arrival was a very special event for them. I followed two years later, the daughter they hoped they would have.

Our home was in the attractive suburb of Waterkloof on the southern outskirts of Pretoria. Together with its slightly more upmarket neighbour, Waterkloof Ridge, this was a suburb of hills and trees, with half-acre lawned properties that were sought after by foreign diplomats. Our house was more modest than most in the suburb, and was extended and altered over the years. The property was a treasure trove for children. We had a very large aviary that you could walk around in, with a bench to sit on. We also had a pond for our family of ducks, and it was a regular thing to wake in the morning to the quacking of Mr and Mrs Duck outside the kitchen door. The backyard had a cricket pitch with nets that doubled as a wall for tennis practice. In front of the house was our narrow, deep swimming pool, where we would gather for morning exercises led enthusiastically by my father. Our driveway was a long sloping one, great for bikes and skateboards. In particular, I loved the garden with its secret spots, ideal for hiding out with my best friends, Helen and Marianne. We were an inseparable trio and our favourite game involved making up stories – 'once upon a time' stories – and acting them out.

My mother's love for animals was passed on to Trevor and I and over the years we had an assortment of dogs, cats and birds. Our much-loved poodle Gypsey and fox terrier Fraser were our regular companions for over a decade, very much part of the fabric of our family. Inevitably several of our precious animals died through illness or misadventure over the years and those were the saddest of days for me. In particular I recall my distress when our poodle puppy fell into the swimming pool and died. I was supposed to have been looking out for him. I cried bitterly too when I rushed out early one winter morning to check up on the newly hatched ducklings, only to find them frozen and lifeless. I gathered them up and took them with me into my own warm bed hoping to revive them, but it was too late.

As the years passed, my parents built a solid financial base. My father had instinctive 'get-up-and-go' qualities and established a thriving real-estate agency business in Pretoria called Herby Currer Pty Ltd. My mother did not return to formal employment after her children arrived; her work was now at home, being a wife and a mother. I did not appreciate until much later in life how frustrating and, indeed, lonely she found this. My mum got on easily with everyone she met. She had a ready laugh and a feisty spirit. For most of my young years, she could not drive a car and felt isolated. The only domestic activity she really enjoyed was cooking. I recall wonderful times with her in the kitchen, measuring out the flour, greasing the pans and, of course, tasting the product, before and after it was put in the oven. She took charge of our evening meals, and each night the four of us would gather around the dining-room table for her casseroles, curries, stews and roasts, followed by jellies, fresh fruit salad and homemade custard. On special occasions we were treated to trifle, lemon meringue pie and her own special milk tart. Dinnertime was the highlight of her day. She had her family around her. She wanted to know what we were up to, and to discuss what was happening in the world.

Holidays were also very important family time. My love for adventurous outdoor holidays comes from my experiences of them as a child. In my and my brother's pre-teen years, with our father in savings mode, we would set off with the dogs and our caravan and head to the sea. Mum would wake us hours before dawn and, armed with blankets and pillows, we would settle in for the long drive. Dad wanted to be at least 200 kilometres away from home before we stopped for breakfast. Three weeks followed of beach cricket, fishing, swimming, picnics and games of all sorts with our new caravan-park friends. At the end of the holiday there would sometimes be a surprise. Instead of going home, Dad would say, 'Why don't we go and spend a few days in Grahamstown, or East London, or Durban?' Off we would go, with fresh excitement for a new adventure.

The best adventures of all were our regular and often impromptu trips to the Kruger National Park, which is, even today, my favourite place for a holiday. Mum and Dad would pick us up from school on a Friday and tell us to jump in – bags were packed, all was set, we were going to the bush. Oh, we loved it. The early-morning starts, the scanning of the bush for animals, the claim and counter-claim of who saw what first, the evening fire, the stars brighter than anything you would see in the city, the stories and the laughter.

Both my father and my mother have passed away – my father prematurely and very sadly from cancer in 1980, and my mother 30 years later at the age of 93. In the 1990s, first my brother, Trevor, and then my husband and I moved to Sydney with our families. Trevor and I are very close. As a surgeon and a banker we have forged ful-filling and rewarding careers. We have followed in the footsteps of our parents by prioritising family above all else. As I see it, there is a lesson in this about the benefits of a strong and stable foundation in life, about the enduring value of being loved as a child.

A few years ago, my husband Allan wrote this poem for our daughter Sharon.

> *On the shoulders of giants,*
> *I've reached this place,*
> *They've borne me strong and true,*
> *And when I reach down,*
> *To lift you up,*
> *I must seem a giant,*
> *To you.*

There is a simple essence in this poem that captures the power of parents. Mine have indeed been giants for me. How lucky am I.

2

LEARNING TO LEARN

Like most kids, I thought about education in terms of what happens at school and at university. I didn't fully appreciate that a quality education involves teaching you to learn, and that learning is a lifelong pursuit.

Having traversed over 60 years of my life, and finding myself learning every step of the way, I know that now. In fact it would be fair to say that there is little that I am more passionate about.

My own educational foundations were rock-solid. Almost all my schooling years were spent at St Mary's Diocesan School for Girls (St Mary's DSG) in Pretoria. Run by the Sisters of the Community of St Mary from Wantage in England, the school was values-based in its approach and largely free from the influence of state. This was important in those years, the 1960s and 1970s, where apartheid[1], the official policy of the National Party government, became fully entrenched. The Population Registration Act of 1950, which required that every South African be classified into one of a number of racial groups, served as the foundation for apartheid. Further laws followed that had the effect of implementing the policy across all areas of economic and social life: job reservation, educational segregation, and the prohibition of marriage and sexual relations between white people and people of colour. Increasingly rigid controls and suppression mechanisms underpinned this construct, together with a powerful propaganda machine. What we read, who we could listen to, what we were taught – the government sought to control it all.

It was lucky for me, therefore, to receive an independent and liberally based education. St Mary's DSG attracted wonderful teachers who freely brought their own philosophies and perspectives into the classroom. Girls attending DSG were taught to think for themselves. We were encouraged to question, to debate, to examine the full facts of any situation. Creativity and outside-the-box thinking were stimulated. We learned to analyse detailed information and to then synthesise the salient points. My love for books, driven firstly by my mother, who had taught me to read before I started school, was further fostered by my truly remarkable English teacher, Mrs Lawrence. Each holiday, she gave us extensive book

---

1   Apartheid literally means 'separation' or 'apart-ness'.

lists with specific questions to ponder. Our horizons widened, our imaginations stirred and our understanding of the world deepened. We learned to have confidence and an independent view. Among others, Mrs Lawrence introduced me to Tolstoy, Dostoevsky, D.H. Lawrence, Eliot and Austen. She brought magic into her classroom as we struggled over *Othello* or *Great Expectations*. We staged mini-dramas of our own, taking parts and playing them out. We set up debates on current-affairs topics. I specifically recall the debate on apartheid, with talented and spirited girls leading the arguments for and against. This open-thinking approach would never have been allowed in government schools of the day.

I also owe my Latin teacher a debt of thanks. Her name was Mrs Van Oudtshoorn, and we held her in great awe. Her requirement was for nothing less than detailed mastery of the structure of the Latin language. Logic and analytical skills were critical tools for success in her classroom, and she painstakingly aided us in their development. Like most things, once you had the basics under control you could start to appreciate the subject. We spent many stimulating hours reflecting upon the ancient world through the texts we studied and the stories we read. Reading around a subject was more than encouraged: it was expected.

For my father, a school education was important but not enough. I was encouraged to do more. What about the piano? I stuck it out for a few years, but even my father realised that it was a lost cause for his daughter. Well, let's try speech and drama. Thursday afternoon after Thursday afternoon, my mother drove me to the home of my teacher. There she and I wrestled with poetry and prose, and how to use the full range of my voice. We practised and practised for the external examinations and eisteddfods, which

I endured each year. I would feel sick with anxiety. I fared best in the prepared delivery of poems and prose; sight-reading was manageable, but performing live and impromptu on given topics filled me with dread. This anxiety carried through to school performances. Being tall in a girls-only school, I was typically assigned male parts. In my final two years, I played Demetrius in Shakespeare's *A Midsummer Night's Dream* and Orlando in *As You Like It*. Although I stepped up willingly, I found these roles challenging. I remember the elaborate costumes, the makeup, the wigs and the boots. I remember the panic of missing my cue and how acutely awkward I felt knowing that beyond the lights were boys from our neighbouring 'brother' school. Drama was not for me. Learning to perform publicly, to project my voice, to use tone and tempo to bring language to life and communicate a message – those benefits escaped me at the time.

I left school in December 1973 without appreciating the powerful gift of learning that I had been receiving. I did not foresee how well it would prepare me for university, for my future career and for life. The truth is that I did not particularly enjoy my school years. Socially, although never ostracised or bullied, I was not one of the popular inner circle of girls. Diligent, hardworking, conscientious, reliable – that was me. In my last year of school, I recall being both excruciatingly bored and absurdly anxious. The boredom was driven by a regime of revision, revision and more revision; the anxiety came from not wanting to let my father down. My final results were good rather than great, but I was on my way. Next stop: the University of Cape Town.

February 1974 and the day of moving away from home arrived. My mother and father took me to the Pretoria train station. They helped me with my bags, held me close and wished me well as I set off on the long 1500-kilometre journey to Cape Town. This was hard for my mother, and tears were not far away, but for me a whole new chapter of life was about to start. At 17 years of age I was both excited and apprehensive. It helped that I was following in the footsteps of my brother and I knew he would look out for me.

My first priority was to make new friends. Fortunately there were many students at my women-only residence, Fuller Hall, who also came from afar and had the same focus. Academically, I set about my arts degree and made the decision to major in Latin and history. I had an early wake-up call in my English 1 class when I failed the mid-year exam, which involved critiquing a poem. I had never failed an exam before. At school, I had received a distinction for English, so failing came as quite a shock. I realised that I had a lot to learn. I was in a challenging tutorial group with extremely bright students and an erudite though rather dismissive lecturer. He told us our life experience was too limited to properly understand poetry. He did, however, provide us with an excellent grounding, and our skills grew. Academically, in this and in other classes I started to mature in my thinking. Learning was exhilarating and, stimulated by like-minded others, I began to find my own voice.

It was in one of the English 1 auditoriums that I first came across my husband-to-be. At the conclusion of a lecture, the class winner of the Chaucer Essay Prize was announced: Allan Kelly. A young man with blond hair stood up. In the style of Rhodesians he had short shorts, a backpack over his shoulder and a friendly, relaxed look about him. It was some months before we actually met, and a few months more before we started dating. Two years later, in December 1976, we became engaged to be married.

In my final year at Fuller Hall, to my great surprise, I was elected by my fellow students to be head student of the residence. It had not entered my mind that I would be considered as the best person for the job. Indeed I had voted for someone else. This was my first significant leadership role, and it carried more responsibility than I was ready for.

That year, 1976, was a year of great change in the country. It was the year of the Soweto uprisings, where black students protesting the use of Afrikaans as the medium of instruction in schools were brutally and shockingly set upon by the police. Rioting and unrest spread around the country, including on the campus of the University of Cape Town.

These were emotional and tense times for students and student leaders. The National Party government's educational policies were, of course, an outrage to me, and I was angry and upset by the events in Soweto. The image of the dying 13-year-old boy, Hector Pieterson, being carried in the arms of a fellow student while his sister ran alongside screaming, will forever remain seared in my memory.[2] I was also deeply worried about the future.

Allan and I had our own small taste of violence and fear when we inadvertently became caught up in a police chase in central Cape Town. On our way through the Adderley Street subway, a small group of black youths running at pace flattened us against the wall. In close pursuit came several armed policemen with dogs. The pounding of feet, the shouting and the barking was already deafening when a tear-gas canister exploded in front of us. I hope I never again experience such panic – the struggle to breathe, the sensation of eyes burning,

---

2   South African photographer Sam Nzima took this iconic image on 16 June 1976, the day the protesting began. It was published on the following day by *The World* newspaper in Johannesburg.

the blind stumbling to find the exit. It was a frightening time.

Over this same period, change was underway at Fuller Hall. Our dining room became the combined dining facility for the students from both Fuller Hall and Smuts Hall, the neighbouring all-male residence. Previous rules of signing male visitors in and out of the residence were superseded by the new reality of many more people coming through the doors early, late, seemingly at all times. The parents of the Fuller Hall students expressed concern, particularly those of first-year students from country towns. The unsettled environment on campus meant that safety and security had become a serious issue. Somehow or other, as leader, I muddled through all of this using a commonsense approach. I asked the students to be alert and watchful for themselves and each other, and to respect the privacy of individuals and the rules of the residence. Fortunately, nothing too serious happened on my watch.

At this point, I was 20 years old. So far, it seemed to me that I had had the best of educations. My future husband would, however, regularly tease me about my arts degree majors, Latin and history:

'Isn't Latin a dead language? What's the point of studying a dead language?'

'As for history, why choose to focus on things that happened in the past?'

Without fail, I would rise to the bait – as I do now. First argument: I loved these subjects. I found them hugely intellectually stimulating. That counts for a lot, doesn't it? Second argument: well, let's take Latin. The words that spring to mind when I think of the skills I developed are analytical thinking, logic, attention to detail, concentration, comprehension, and problem solving.

And what about the beauty of the language itself, including the immense pleasure of understanding words and their derivations? For example, I love knowing that the word 'miracle' comes from the Latin word *mirus*, meaning 'wonderful'; that 'integrity' is derived from *integer*, meaning 'whole'; and that 'companion' comes from *com* and *panis*, meaning 'together with bread'. Next argument: history. This is not just studying the past – it is seeking to understand what occurred, and why. It involves research, interpretation, the synthesis of information, the contemplation of different schools of thought. It is about people and leadership and philosophy, and helps in our understanding of today's world.

Years later, when I started out on my Master of Business Administration (MBA), I was intimidated by the mostly engineers, chartered accountants, mathematicians and doctors in the group. Yet when it came to the cut and thrust of things, I found that I could write clearly and concisely and could argue the merits of a case. I could look at a complex situation from many points of view, getting to grips with the details while also standing back and thinking strategically about the whole. Thanks to my early experiences of leadership, I could work effectively within a group, as a team member or as team leader. In short, I believe my liberal arts and classical background served me very well.

Having made a case for this type of education, let me now further the case for education in general.

Education is transformative in its power. For nations, an educated workforce drives productivity and innovation, supporting future prosperity.

To parents prioritising and investing in education – what powerful springboards you are establishing for your children.

Teachers, we owe you a huge debt of thanks. Your demanding roles are frequently undervalued, yet your care and professionalism help shape young minds and hearts.

Organisations, big and small, you are crucial in assisting employees to develop the skills required for productive work. As needs change, as new technologies emerge, make sure you help your people learn afresh.

Students, whatever your age, and wherever you are, grab the educational opportunities coming your way with both hands. Keep being curious about the world. Learn to learn. Learn to love learning. It will change your life – it's done that for me.

3

CHOOSE TO
BE POSITIVE

I recently came across the Oprah Winfrey book *What I Know For Sure*. In her introduction, Oprah describes how, when promoting the 1998 film *Beloved*, the television interviewer and film critic Gene Siskel asked her, as a final, perhaps throwaway question, what it was that she knew for sure. At the time Oprah was at a loss for words, but in the years ahead it became a central question of her life.

And so I ask myself the same question: what is it that I know for sure? What do I know – really know – that has stood the test of time?

I have at least one answer: I know for sure that if you bring a positive attitude to life, you will be happier. Others around you will be happier, too.

I had an early role model to learn from: my father. He was a tall man with a strong build, eyes that sparkled, and a wide, friendly smile. His disposition was a naturally optimistic one. As a top-class sportsman, he combined physical talent with hard work and mental strength. On the sports field, he had the ability to focus 100 per cent and yet remain relaxed. His football career had revealed his remarkable talent. Later in life, he switched to lawn bowls, winning five South African championship medals, two gold and three silver. In 1950, at the Empire Games in Auckland, he and his fellow bowlers won the gold medal in the foursomes event. His hand–eye coordination skills and excellent temperament meant that he excelled in most sports. He played scratch golf and, annoyingly, would easily beat me at my own game – tennis. He loved competing; he loved sport in all its forms. Dad's philosophy was a simple one – if you work hard and apply yourself intelligently to the task, you will be rewarded with superior results. In fact, you will be amazed at how lucky you become!

My brother and I were the prime recipients of Dad's tried-and-tested wisdom. The occasion of the big tennis match, or major exam, or end-of-year school play inevitably involved a prepping session.

I recall a particular Saturday afternoon. My tennis match in the local club championship was about to get underway and the conditions were challenging – it was hot and dry with swirling winds, which was unusual for Pretoria. 'Right,' my father said as we drove to the venue, 'just remember you've done the hard work. You are ready for this. These conditions are perfect for your game. Your first serve is so consistent, and your forehand drive is flat and fast.' The truth is that my 'consistent' first serve lacked power and my 'flat and fast' forehand drive lacked topspin. But for my father, the objective was always to find the positive, to help build confidence and self-belief. This was his way – to set out expecting the best, to be prepared to invest every ounce of effort, to never be defeatist. My brother and I knew that nothing would upset him more than our giving up or behaving badly. 'Just give it your best. Make sure you try. Relax. Relax your shoulders,' are words that still ring in my ears today.

My father applied this 'choosing to be positive' attribute to all elements of his life. It was wonderful to see how much joy and satisfaction he got out of even the most ordinary things. He exuded energy and took difficulties and challenges in his stride. Things that didn't go to plan became learning opportunities. What needed to be done next was what became important. Not surprisingly, people gravitated to his warmth and enthusiasm. In fact, people loved my father. They knew he would go the extra mile to help them. He was a natural leader.

In September 1980, at 64 years of age, this very important person in our family died. The diagnosis of cancer six months earlier had come as a major shock to my mother, my brother and to me. The period between April and September was extremely distressing. It was a time of intense pain and sadness. Dad's form of cancer was a rare sarcoma. By the time it was diagnosed, it was inoperable, and the malignancy from the primary tumour under his left armpit soon spread to his lungs and his liver. He experienced extreme pain and it was difficult for us to watch his rapid physical deterioration.

In the last month he struggled to stand up, let alone walk. Eating became a major challenge. The chemotherapy and radiation treatment he received caused severe nausea and discomfort but did nothing to slow the spread of the disease.

I was 24 years old and living in Johannesburg with Allan. Trevor lived in Cape Town with his wife, Janet, and their baby daughter, Cathy. Each evening I travelled the 65 kilometres to Pretoria to be with my mother and father, and early each morning I returned to Johannesburg for work. At night in my bed in our Waterkloof home, I wept. The tears just kept coming. I was upset, I was sad, I was angry. Why should this happen to my father? He was a fit and healthy man, he had not smoked for over 30 years, he was full of life and energy, he took care of himself. He used to return from his annual trips to the doctor boasting that his heart was as strong as an ox and that he had the physical fitness level of a 25-year-old.

Only the year before, he had retired and sold his real-estate business. Now was the time that he and Mum were going to use their savings, travel and enjoy the next phase of their lives. The long-planned post-retirement trip to Australia had been scheduled, with the first stop in Adelaide to visit his brother Norman, then on to Melbourne, Sydney, Brisbane, Cairns and Alice Springs. My father was very excited. He told us later that it was on the day of boarding the plane in March 1980 that he had first felt the lump under his armpit.[3] Four weeks later, in significant pain, he visited a medical centre in Cairns. 'You need to get on a plane and return to South Africa as soon as possible' was what the doctor told him. Allan and I collected Mum and Dad from Johannesburg

---

3   Late in the previous year, my father had developed severe shoulder and neck pain. This was misdiagnosed at the time as being due to a prolapsed disc in his cervical spine, possibly from years of heading a football. An operation to fuse the vertebrae in his neck was performed. The pain persisted, however, and the undiagnosed tumour continued to grow and spread.

International Airport. It was extremely upsetting to see my father emerge from the plane in a wheelchair. Six months later, he died in our Pretoria home.

This story is painful for me to tell. I relay it in this chapter named 'Choose to be Positive' because throughout this period, notwithstanding the shock and the personal sadness that my father would have felt, this is exactly what he did. He worked hard at being 100 per cent in the moment, fighting the disease with all his strength. He never gave into despair or indulged in self-pity. When it was clear that nothing could be done to halt its course, he turned his full attention to caring for us. He encouraged us to be grateful for all the happiness and joy in our lives; he told us, together and individually, how much he loved us and how proud he was of the family. He reflected on his life and said how lucky he had been. He was excited about our futures and had plenty of ideas to offer. He told us not to be sad.

A special evening in my life is the night before he died. Dad wanted to die in his own home, and his bed was placed right in the middle of the living room, in the centre of activity. Somehow, that night, the pain receded. Dad sat up in his bed, ate yoghurt from a tub and joked with us. We laughed and cried together. At a point in the evening, he called Allan and me to his side. He put our heads together, held our hands and said, 'I know you two will be happy together. Look after each other. I am very proud of you.'

We scattered my father's ashes on his beloved farm north of Pretoria. I think of him often, and of the many life lessons I learned from him. That you can choose your attitude to things is among the most important. It is something that I know for sure, and its impact on me continues today.

On many occasions over my career, I have returned home stressed and exhausted from the difficulties of a tough day. As I drive into the garage and park the car, I can feel the tension in my shoulders. I may be annoyed, frustrated, stressed or a mix of all three. But before I get out of the vehicle, I force myself to stop and reflect. Just as I have taken care during the day to respond professionally and constructively to the issues, no matter how difficult they have been, so too must I take care to choose the attitude and spirit I bring into my home. Will I make my husband and children the victims of my difficult day? Will I have lots to say about wet towels on the floor, dishes unwashed and homework not done, with the result that everyone runs for cover? Or will I make the necessary mental adjustment and bring positive energy, a happy voice, a smiling face, into my home?

I can choose. It is a powerful thing to know.

4

LOVE WHAT
YOU DO

This is what I have learned:
- You only live once.
- You owe it to yourself to be happy.
- To be happy you need to find meaning in what you do, and you need to love it.
- If you love what you do, you will grow in confidence, your skill sets will strengthen, and you will deliver.
- You will love what you do even more.

- You will be enthusiastic about new opportunities.
- You will cope better with setbacks.
- Your happiness will spill over to all elements of your life.
- You will keep learning.

On the other hand:
- If you find yourself unhappy for a protracted period in your work, or in your life, you need to make a change.
- Consider first whether it is your own attitude you need to change, whether you are choosing to find fault and allowing yourself to be continuously negative.
- But perhaps it is not your attitude.
- It is the work itself, work that does not play to your strengths, work that is causing you ever-increasing stress, with your confidence falling and your self-esteem eroding.
- Perhaps it is the person you work for, or the team you work with, resulting in you feeling unsupported, undermined, or diminished.
- Work out what it is that is driving your unhappiness.
- And make the right change.
- Don't wait for someone to make a decision for you.
- Don't just hope things will get better.
- They usually get worse.
- Make your own call on what is required.
- Then do it.

Love what you do.
It really matters.

I did not learn this all at once of course. What happened was that in my early twenties, I had an experience that propelled me up the learning curve. Fiercely unhappy as a government schoolteacher in Johannesburg, I made a change to financial services. There was a certain randomness to landing up in the banking world, but I found that I loved it. It became my career, and a very important part of my life.

Even before commencing at university, I had decided that I wanted to be a schoolteacher. No doubt my own schooling had something to do with this, as well as my love for books and my passion for learning. I knew that my father would have liked me to choose something less traditional; we had many a conversation when he would tell me I could do whatever I wanted – medicine, engineering, law. This was the time of Neil Armstrong taking man's first steps on the moon, and I recall my father saying, 'You could be an astronaut.' None of that swayed me from my enthusiasm to teach, and continuing on at the University of Cape Town after my arts degree, I completed a one-year diploma course for secondary-school teaching. Latin and history were my chosen subjects.

I absolutely loved my early experiences of teaching. As a student teacher in Cape Town I completed four week-long blocks at Sea Point Boys' High School, at Bishops and at an Afrikaans boys' school in the Pinelands area. Teaching history in Afrikaans to 16-year-olds was certainly well out of my comfort zone. Thankfully, the boys were extraordinarily polite.

My first formal post began in January 1978 as a Latin teacher at Falcon College in Rhodesia, a country that was then well on the path to becoming Zimbabwe. It was a privilege to teach at an outstanding school that was widely respected throughout the country.

Falcon College is a boys' boarding school situated in the bush, about 50 kilometres outside of Bulawayo. As the only Latin teacher at the school, I had a lot of responsibility. My major role was to prepare the boys for the important 'O', 'M' and 'A' level examinations.[4] Once again I found myself deeply immersed in the subject, and I loved it. My classes were small – I had around 16 O-level boys, six M-level and only three A-level. The boys were without exception intelligent and hardworking. I didn't know it then, but this was teaching at its very best. Being a bush school, I lived in my own house on the property and was warmly welcomed into the community. On a personal level I was very happy too – Allan and I were newly married and, although he was away a lot completing 12 months' compulsory military service in a country engaged in a civil war, we were excited about our future together.

Less than 18 months later, we moved to Johannesburg. Influenced by his training and experience as a medic while in the Rhodesian Army, Allan had decided to build on his social-work degree and become a doctor. He commenced the six-year period of study at the University of the Witwatersrand, and I needed to find a job. This proved to be more difficult than expected. No posts were available at any of the private schools, and in government schools I faced the disadvantage of being a married woman and therefore only being able to be employed on a temporary basis. Twenty-four hours was all the notice I would receive should a male or an unmarried female teacher become available. And even then, I was required to obtain my husband's permission to teach. Allan thought that was very entertaining; I, on the other hand, was highly indignant.

---

4   Falcon College uses the Cambridge International Examinations Curriculum, which, at that time, included examinations at O-level (Ordinary level) and at A-level (Advanced level). M-level (Matriculation level) sat between the two.

We needed the income, so the form was signed and I commenced at Highlands North Boys' High School. Although appointed to teach Latin, on my arrival I was informed that things had changed and I would now be teaching English and religious instruction. The fact that I was not qualified to teach either seemed not to matter. I was assigned 'lower stream' classes, and for the first time I encountered students who had no interest in learning. Some had failed repeatedly and were extremely disruptive, even violent, in the classroom. I tried disciplining them, with no success; I tried inspiring them, with even less success. In my naivety and youthfulness, I thought they might respond to one of the poems I had most loved in my school days at St Mary's DSG. Called 'The Horses of the Camargue', it is lilting in its beauty and throbbing in its rhythms. I typed the poem out at home, made copies and handed them to the class. I then introduced the poem, explaining its context and outlining what to look for. I began to read it aloud to capture the rising tempo, the untamed wildness of these beautiful horses. Not far in, the poem came back to me in the form of flying paper aeroplanes. Oh dear. I was well out of my depth and I was struggling alone.

That post lasted a term. My next one, at a boys' senior school in Randburg, also lasted a term. Here I taught history to each of the ten classes making up the Year 7 cohort. The average size of each class was around 30 and it was difficult to get to know individual boys. The curriculum was fixed, methodologies were standardised, and the head of the department told me that I should stick to the script. Again I struggled with engaging the pupils, and again I struggled with discipline. Every day became an ordeal. I would board my bus to school in the morning and dream a little dream of it breaking down so that I could be late, or perhaps even miss school for the day. I doubted myself, lost confidence, lost weight, and became steadily more unhappy.

The day arrived when I realised just how bad things had become. It was a spring afternoon and I was on duty for the sports activities of the day. At 5 p.m., tired and generally miserable, I closed up the school clubhouse and set off down the stairs for the bus stop. A young boy, 13 or 14 years old at most, ran towards me, asking urgently, 'Please, ma'am, may I collect my blazer? I think I left it inside.' I visibly displayed my annoyance, turned around, walked back up the stairs, reopened the door and, with my hand on my hip, gave him a lecture. 'You need to think ahead and take better care of your things,' I said. 'Don't let this happen again. Be quick – you are holding me up.'

Once he had come and gone, I stood still for a moment and felt suddenly ashamed. What had happened to me that I was behaving in this way? Where was that positive disposition, that friendly person who likes children? It was clear that something needed to change, and that I was the one who must make that change. I realised it would not be fixed by moving schools again – it was a matter of leaving teaching.

I had no idea what I was going to do. I recall sitting on the floor in my mother's bedroom, wallowing in self-pity. My mum, in her no-nonsense way, told me to snap out of it, while my father, in his practical make-it-happen way, set about opening some doors. As part of his real-estate business in Pretoria, he ran an agency for the South African Permanent Building Society (SA Perm).[5] A call or two later and I had an appointment with a manager at the SA Perm

---

5   SA Perm was merged with Nedbank in 1988 to form the Nedcor Group.

in Johannesburg. I was by no means sure that this was the type of work I wanted to do, and I am certain they were doubtful that this young woman with her Latin and history qualifications was right for them. What I remember most clearly about the interview was the comment: 'Well, we'll have to see. It may be possible for you to become a supervisor one day.'

On 14 January 1980, I started as a teller in the Simmonds Street branch in the centre of Johannesburg. From the very first day, I was happier. This was partly due to having a completely different type of job, one in which I quickly found my feet. The pressures of my everyday teaching life fell away, my mind was engaged in new learning, and bit by bit my confidence re-emerged. What I particularly enjoyed was spending time with customers and trying to help them. I found the variety in the role stimulating, and I loved being part of a team. Because I was eager and hardworking, I was given additional opportunities to learn. Within a matter of months, I had been selected as a participant in the Perm's inaugural Accelerated Training Program. Over a three-year period, each participant would rotate through the various divisions of the organisation, receiving on-the-job and classroom training as well as individualised coaching. Only a handful of people were chosen from across the company for this accelerated development, and I was lucky to be one of them.

This all-round grounding was extremely valuable. Many companies today offer similar opportunities in the form of graduate programs – something I strongly encourage. In my case, not only was it stimulating and fun, but it set me up for a longer-term career in the industry. I welcomed the exposure to so many parts of the business and was able to identify the types of work I loved best.

On the personal front, Allan was delighted that he had his positive, energetic wife back. Life was good.

I have a further story to tell about making a change. In a career, it may happen that you are in the right industry, even in the right company, but the circumstances of your work are such that you no longer love what you do. It could be that you are overwhelmed with pressure. Your skill set may be a poor fit for the role; you and your manager may not see eye to eye. Whatever the circumstances, if over a protracted period you find yourself unhappy and stressed, wishing the days are over before they begin, something needs to change. It is important that you identify what it is and then make the change.

My story relates to my early years in Australian banking. In this case, it was not the industry, it was not the company and it was definitely not my manager. In a nutshell, I was struggling to cope with the volume and complexity of issues on my plate. I was making mistakes at work, and was exhausted and stressed at home.

Allan and I had been in Australia with our young family for close to two years. The year was 1999 and I was working at the Commonwealth Bank as General Manager, Strategic Marketing. Allan was dealing with the multiple exhausting steps of requalifying as a medical practitioner and paediatrician in Australia, and our four children were settling in to their different schools. It was probably the most challenging time for us as a family. We were in a new country, we were finding our way in how to get things done, the children were young, and Allan and I were both stretched in setting up new careers.

While I can only compliment and thank the Commonwealth Bank for the significant help they gave us in making the transition, it was still very hard. My role was a new one in the bank, established as part of a fundamentally different operating model that David Murray, the CEO, was putting into place. At my request, my responsibilities included the leadership of the bank's card business. As it turned out, this was the straightforward element of the job. Having accountability for the bank's retail distribution and payments strategies was more challenging, particularly as the role involved the negotiation and establishment of various third-party partnerships. The most notable of these was Woolworths Ezy Banking, a new retail banking business that we launched with Australian retailer, Woolworths. Further, the dotcom boom was underway, with several new internet-based companies setting up unique business models, introducing both threats and opportunities for existing players. It was a rapidly developing area, and strategically very important.

I had an excellent team around me and lots of support from John Mulcahy, the group executive of Australian Financial Services, to whom I reported; yet I was exhausted, totally depleted, and struggling to manage the extensive workload. Weekend after weekend I would head into the office to try to stay on top of things. The result: stress at home and guilt for not being the mum I wanted to be, and pressure at work with a few too many balls being dropped. I could not go on like this – something needed to change.

After deep consideration, I fronted up to John to discuss the situation and propose a solution. I told him the job had become too big for one general manager and suggested that my role be split in two. I would retain the core elements of cards, payments and distribution, while a talented executive who reported to me, Bernadette Inglis, could be appointed as general manager for the growing dotcom/internet area. While this was the perfect solution, it is not one that executives readily come up with. It is rare for leaders to propose that their roles be reduced: leaders often make the mistake of measuring themselves and their importance by the size of their position, how many functions it includes, the number of people and dollars involved.

Intuitively I knew that what mattered for my career success and personal happiness was doing my job well – all elements of it. To achieve that, the scope of the role needed to change. John agreed, my job was halved, Bernadette was appointed and I got my life back. Having been in a vicious circle, the virtuous circle now kicked in – happier person, performance improved, confidence, energy and engagement lifted.

By far the most demanding role of my executive career was my last one, CEO of Westpac. At times, the exhaustion and stress showed in my eyes and in my face. It was a highly visible position, both complex and challenging. Like any role, it had elements that were frustrating and others that simply had to be endured. It would be true to say, however, that of all my roles, it was the one that I cherished most. I was deeply aware of the privilege of the position and keenly understood the responsibilities that came with it. I loved the real opportunity to make a difference. The job of CEO is a leadership one, and it was the leadership elements that I particularly loved – the building of a team, the work on meaning and purpose for the company, the slow but sure embedding of a culture centred on customers, the focus on diversity, the management of change.

There is no doubt that I finished up a better leader than I started. This is as it should be. Part of 'loving what you do' is to keep learning, keep practising, keep listening, keep assessing and reassessing. It involves refreshing yourself and the agenda, building on what's working and stepping up again. It's also good to stand still and reflect for a moment on the journey thus far. I found that checking off milestones gave me fresh energy for what lay ahead.

A few years ago, I caught up with a fellow CEO of a global top-20 banking institution in the days immediately after he had stepped down from his role. I congratulated him and asked him how he was feeling. 'Well,' he said, 'let me answer your question this way. It's like having a boat. The best two days are the day you buy it and the day you sell it.'

I'm glad that this was not true for me.

5

BE BOLD, DIG DEEP, BACK YOURSELF

When you are a senior executive in a large and well-performing company, people assume that you are always confident and across the issues, that you know exactly what you want to do and how to do it. Well, in my case, that was not true. I can recall many, many moments of doubt, uncertainty, fear of failure, fear of being inadequate. In her excellent book *Lean In*, Sheryl Sandberg asks her readers to consider the question of what they would do if they were not afraid. The question strikes a chord with me.

The fact is that in the really big 'fork-in-the-road' decisions, I stared into my fears and insecurities and pushed myself hard to get beyond them. I learned that, as challenging as it may be, it pays to be courageous and back yourself. I have been encouraged by others – sometimes strongly encouraged – to have a go. It has helped to be aware of the many people who will support and assist along the way.

While there is no doubt that fears of failure and inadequacy can affect both men and women, they would seem, as Sandberg discusses in her book, to be a particular issue for women. This is my experience too. Over my career, I have observed that women tend to be harder on themselves in terms of their readiness for a next move. They are more likely to wait to be approached for a promotion than to seek it out, and less likely to negotiate on their pay.

As more women occupy executive and board positions, and as awareness and support grow, this situation is improving. Books like Sandberg's really help. But at that very personal and individual level, when confronted with a big decision requiring courage and boldness and pushing past your fears, it is not easy.

I could give any one of a number of stories of my own 'digging deep' battles. The decision Allan and I made to leave our home in South Africa and start afresh in Australia with our four young children involved courage and confronting fears of making the wrong choice. Putting my hand up for the role of CEO of St.George, and then accepting the position once it was offered, brought much soul-searching: 'Am I ready? Can I do this?' Similarly, when I was appointed CEO of Westpac, I was forced to confront an array of self-doubts and anxieties. As the global financial crisis got underway, these magnified.

The story I will more fully explore, however, is of something that occurred earlier in my career, providing a stepping stone and point of learning for subsequent life and career decisions.

By 1992, allowing for two pregnancies and four children as well as an 18-month MBA study break, I had been working within financial services in Johannesburg for 12 years. My role was General Manager, Human Resources (HR) for the Perm. It was a very exciting time to be in human resources, after the release of Nelson Mandela from jail, the return of political exiles, and new programs of reconstruction and development. The group was also undergoing structural change, with centralisation of functions such as HR, finance and IT. In the proposed new model for HR, I set my sights on a role 'in the centre' with, all going well, a longer-term pathway to potentially becoming the group general manager for the function.

The bank's executive leadership, however, had different ideas, and I was summoned to the office of the group CEO and managing director, Richard Laubscher. Fronting up involved the first piece of courage. Richard then outlined the possibility of my heading up the group's card division, a largely standalone business of about 1000 people. My immediate response was to say that I knew very little about the card business or card technology, and to ask Richard what was involved. He rattled off words such as 'issuing', 'acquiring' and 'merchant interchange', which were all new for me, and said, 'Don't worry – you'll learn.' He asked me to go away and reflect and then let him know if I was interested.

It didn't take long for me to work out all the reasons why this would be a very risky thing to do, why doing this job was impossible, why I was doomed to fail. I wrote them down:

- I had no experience running a profit-and-loss business.
- I had no experience in technology.
- I would be coming into this position from the HR world, which was perceived at the time as a 'soft' function.
- I would be coming from the 'taken-over' entity in the bank, which looked after what was seen as the 'less-sophisticated' building-society activities of savings and loans.
- I would be the only woman at this level in the bank, and the only woman running a profit-and-loss business.
- Allan and I had four children. Sharon was five years old. The triplets, Sean, Mark and Annie, were two.
- Allan had a full-time role working as a paediatrician at Baragwanath Hospital in Soweto.

I have to say, even now I wonder, what was Richard thinking?

I also recognised that this was a breakthrough opportunity. Running a business with all the elements of sales, marketing, customer relationships, risk, operations, technology and strategy was a very exciting prospect. From my very first day in the business, I would be its leader.

In this decision, as in all of my big life decisions, the person who helped me most to dig deep and to back myself was my husband, Allan.

On the issue of 'Can I do this job?', he commented: 'You'll never know unless you try.'

On the issue of 'What if I fail?', his answer was: 'Well, Richard doesn't think you will, or he wouldn't offer you the job.'

On the issue of 'How will we cope?', he said, 'Oh, we'll manage somehow – we always do.'

And so I said yes. I knew that I was in for a rollercoaster ride of learning, of failing, of once again digging deep and picking myself up again. I knew I would have to keep being courageous. But to really step up in my leadership journey, even though I was afraid, I needed to say yes.

I am sometimes asked: 'If you could provide just one piece of advice to young women as they set out in their careers, what would it be?' My answer is always the same: back yourself, dig deep, and have a go – not just for those big fork-in-the-road decision points, but for elements of your everyday life.

To return to the key question of what I would do if I were not afraid, here's a small list to reflect on.

If I were not afraid:

- I would be my own advocate for that key leadership role I'm aspiring to, even though I know I have lots to learn and that I am not 100 per cent ready.
- I would not let myself off the hook by saying I don't have the experience or the skills to step up and deliver.
- I would volunteer to do the presentation to the executive team, or at the board meeting.
- I would speak out on behaviour from colleagues that is sexist or racist or demeaning to others.
- I would be honest with my boss and my colleagues about how I feel.
- I would ask for more help.
- I would say that I don't understand, could you please explain again.
- I would raise my hand and ask the speaker the question on my mind.

- I would not retreat if I was being ignored or dismissed.
- I would not allow myself to be 'spoken over'.
- I would care less about what others think.
- I would fight for equal treatment with my male colleagues.
- I would fight for equal pay.

Fear of failure, fear of being embarrassed, fear of being found wanting, of being socially awkward, of being thought to be stupid, of looking like you don't belong – these are paralysing fears. I have faced them and have got better at staring them down. I have learned to ask for help and to willingly accept it. I have learned to be less perfectionist and less defensive. I have become more comfortable with my own judgements.

It takes courage to back yourself. Please do it. Please give yourself a chance.

PART II

LEADERSHIP

Lessons, insights,
perspectives

I

RIGHT PEOPLE,
RIGHT ROLES

Jim Collins in his book *Good to Great* captures a crucial lesson. A key conclusion of his detailed five-year study into what makes good companies become great was that good-to-great leaders '*first* got the right people on the bus, the wrong people off the bus, and the right people in the right seats'. First the people, then the direction. He adds: 'People are *not* your most important asset. The *right* people are.'

Most people nod their heads and say yes, that makes sense. The challenge for the leader is to consistently deliver on each of the critical elements: have a clear understanding of what designates 'right' and 'wrong'; select rigorously for 'right' and ensure 'wrong' are replaced; assign the roles according to skills and strengths. This takes discipline, judgement and courage, coupled with a healthy dose of self-awareness and the ability to face facts.

In the previous chapter 'Be Bold, Dig Deep, Back Yourself', I outlined the circumstances of my appointment in 1992 to general manager of Nedcor Bank's card division. It was my first senior executive position, one I was catapulted into without preparation. My mandate was to drive change in the business, introduce a freshness of style, innovate around products and processes, and bring into being a customer-service culture. All my Wits Business School MBA training of 1985–86 was going to be put into practice. I had no real idea of how I was going to do it, but I intuitively knew where to start. With the people.

Just for a moment, let me put myself in the shoes of the existing senior leadership team of the business. They had suddenly and unexpectedly lost their longstanding boss; each of them was deeply experienced in the credit card industry – in fact, most had been part of the team who established the business in the late 1970s; they were all men (of course); and most had Afrikaans as their first language.

Suddenly they had a new, much younger leader thrust upon them who, apart from having no experience in the industry, was different in so many ways. It is understandable that resistance was high. Getting out of an elevator one day, I overheard the *sotto voce* comment: 'She won't last long.'

It was imperative and urgent that I make changes. *Good to Great* had not yet been written, but somehow or other I set about doing exactly what Collins advocates.

Within months, with lots of help and support from my own boss, Mike Leeming, I introduced four new executives to the business and agreed with three existing employees that it was time for them to leave.

Each new team member was carefully selected. It was critical I find executives with experience in the industry, as mine was non-existent and those with current experience were on their way out the door. I also needed capability in technology, expertise in corporate banking, and financial management skills. First and foremost, however, I chose people who were excited by the challenge and the opportunity, who were team players, who were prepared to work hard and whom I believed I could trust and rely upon. Not always in my career have I chosen well, but this time I did. And changes within the organisation began. Together we figured out the strategy for the business – where we wanted the bus to go. A new culture of collaboration and teamwork, and of treating people with respect, began to infuse the business. Delivering great service to customers became our call to action. As a team, we learned how to best combine and leverage the individual strengths we brought. It was my first experience of a team where each member understood that his or her role was to do whatever was required to ensure that together, we delivered. We certainly made mistakes – some quite substantial – and we learned from them. It was exciting and fun.

By 1997, the business was very different from what it had been in 1992. We had substantially grown our market share while improving the customer-service experience. Our financial performance was strong.

Looking back now, I appreciate that there was a fair bit of good fortune in landing the right people for the right roles at that time.

It was also quite straightforward to manage the departures of the existing leadership. If I was going to stay, they wanted to go. Achieving all elements of this formula – right people on, right roles assigned, wrong people off – proved to be critical to our success.

In terms of selection, my experience has taught me this:

- Selection matters a lot. Who you bring on board and who you promote are among the most important decisions you will make as a leader.

- Take time to identify the right person. Don't fall into the trap of yielding to the pressure of 'I really need to fill this position. John Smith is available and he will be okay.' Okay is not good enough. If you are not sure, don't appoint. Keep looking, even if it takes longer than others think reasonable.

- The quality of the next level of management is hugely impacted by the selection decisions you make. 'A' players tend to attract and appoint 'A' players for their teams; 'B' players tend to set their sights lower. Poor selection decisions have multiplier effects.

- Select first for attitude and for values alignment. I look for people who are enthusiastic and have a positive frame of reference. I want people who like people and who are team players. Being smart, flexible and results-oriented also counts for a lot. Pass these tests and then I will move to assess fit for the skill set required.

- Be prepared to take chances on people, young people for example, who, in addition to being smart, have shown great promise. Back them up with support, providing feedback and encouragement. It is immensely rewarding to see them learn and grow.

- Be upfront about the challenges of the job. It is a mistake to downplay the likely issues, frustrations and pressure points. The interview conversation is an early step in setting up a relationship of openness and trust.
- Make sure you reference-check thoroughly, and not only with the referee names provided by the candidate. I have found that the best predictor of success is past track record. What has the candidate achieved and how did he or she go about it? How did they deal with pressure, with things not going their way? Obtain real examples and honest assessments from people who have observed past performance firsthand.
- If you make a selection mistake – right person, wrong role or simply wrong person – act quickly. Hoping the situation improves while making excuses for poor performance is not a successful strategy; it is an avoidance strategy that soaks up your energy. Dealing with it quickly is fairest to the individual, too.

In terms of 'right roles', key lessons I have learned are:
- Put individuals in roles where they can play to their strengths. This is the best way to help them flourish and achieve. They will grow in confidence and mature in their capabilities.
- In some cases, shaping or adapting the role to suit the individual is required. This is contrary to the classic HR approach of – define the structure, establish the job description, create the 'person specification' and then select for it. But it works. Structures and roles need to be able to flex.

- While I recommend being careful on this one, I have on various occasions brought wonderfully talented individuals on board without specific roles being available. When doing this, I have found that it is best to have a gameplan in mind that can be clearly communicated and executed in reasonably short order. What you don't want is existing team members feeling threatened or distracted.
- While exposing up-and-coming executives to different parts of the business is highly desirable, in my experience rotating very senior executives in and out of roles in order for them to gain additional breadth and experience requires great care. I have seen competent executives moved into roles for which they were not suited and which they did not enjoy. Confidence erodes and performance falls. It is hard to fix.

With regard to the 'wrong people off the bus' part of the equation, here are my learnings:

- A team member who is misaligned in terms of values and behaviours needs to be dealt with, regardless of the strength of his or her bottom-line contribution. It could be that the individual is undermining of the leader and the leader's agenda. He or she is cynical, selfish, contemptuous of others and fails to search for common ground. Behaviours such as this cannot be tolerated. In fact they are dangerous to the leader and poisonous for the organisation. Dealing with such an individual is not easy. You might find yourself delaying as you reflect on what else you could do to change this untenable situation. Ultimately, biting the bullet is what it takes. Despite an invariably difficult and stressful conversation with an executive who may be angry or emotional, relief is what you will soon feel – your own and that of the team around you. A year or two down the track and you will wonder why it took you so long.

- Then there is the executive who meets behavioural and ethical standards yet over a period consistently fails on performance. I have found that in this tough scenario, the difficulty of the 'off the bus' conversation is inversely proportionate to the extent and quality of the feedback and support the individual has received over the preceding period. Indeed it is related to the nature of the relationship and the degree of trust that exists between the leader and the executive. Further, while the decision is a necessary one, it is very important that the leader recognise its impact on the individual and on his or her family. Thoughtfulness and respect are required. Give the executive time to work through the next steps. Involve them in the broader communication of the decision. Be careful of overzealous HR, IT or security functions that abruptly shut down passwords, de-activate access codes and require the return of corporate cards. Don't let the experience of years of loyal service be spoiled in this way.
- Sometimes it happens that a trusted and loyal executive is no longer 'in the right role' because the role has changed and different skills are required. I have found that it is best to tackle this head-on, and early, as, quite aside from hampering the progress of the business, it is unfair and disrespectful to the loyal executive. Very soon the problem will become clear to all. Early and frank conversations

provide the best chance of identifying an alternative role, possibly at a lower level. Even without that option, it pays the executive the respect of letting him or her own and manage the situation with dignity.

- A final point: whatever the reason or circumstances precipitating the exit, the leader must take on the situation herself. Face-to-face conversation, not delegated to the HR team – nothing less will do. Prepare properly, put yourself in the other's shoes, be fair, thoughtful and professional. These situations are tough. They take courage, and exact an emotional toll. The mark of a good leader is that she does this well.

In his bus analogy, Collins makes the point that the 'good-to-great' companies first got the right people on and the wrong people off, and only then figured out where to drive it: first the people, then the direction. While this may sound simple, and easy to do, in practice I have found the complexity of implementation considerable. The situation of the business at the time, the external environment, specific factors surrounding my appointment as leader – all needed to be taken into consideration. The best examples I can use to amplify this are my two CEO experiences.

The search for the new St.George Bank leader was initiated as a result of the sudden death of its CEO, Ed O'Neal, in September 2001. While the bank was performing soundly, it was widely expected, including by the executives within the company, that St.George would be acquired by one of the major banks in the foreseeable future. As a result of the government's four pillars policy, the four major banks were precluded from merging with each other.

St.George was Australia's fifth-largest bank. Established in 1937 in the suburbs of southern Sydney as a building society, it had grown through mergers and in 1992 achieved full banking status. Ten years later, on 1 July 2002, its restrictive articles of association, effectively precluding any takeover, were due to expire. As a preparatory move, both National Australia Bank and ANZ had acquired close to 10 per cent stakes in St.George, the maximum allowable at that time. ANZ divested its stake in March 2001, which left National Australia Bank as the most likely aggressor. In setting out to find a successor to Ed, the St.George board was keen to identify a leader who could quickly define and articulate an independent growth agenda for the bank, and achieve strong share-price appreciation. As I discuss in the chapter 'A Woman in Business', both the market and I were surprised that I was selected for this task. By the time I commenced, on 14 January 2002, the bank had been without a CEO for four months and was less than six months away from the 1 July D-day.

Coming into this situation, I needed to move quickly on a number of fronts – understanding the bank's strengths and its opportunities, getting to grips with its defence strategy, and assessing its leadership. I soon recognised that I needed to inject new skills and fresh energy while simultaneously drawing upon the experience of those around me. Both change and stability were important. Within a matter of weeks I made my first appointment, that of Peter Clare as my new head of strategy. Peter and I had worked closely together at the Commonwealth Bank and I knew that he would bring valuable 'make-it-happen' skills and a strong commercial approach. Over the next few months I made a number of further changes, appointing Andrew Thorburn as group executive for personal banking, and Rob Chapman to the position of managing director, Bank of South Australia. Again, I had worked closely with both of them at the Commonwealth Bank. I understood their capabilities and their potential, and knew I could trust them. Culturally, they would fit very well within St.George, being strongly people and customer-service oriented. My final key appointment was that of Paul Fegan, a respected senior banker at National Australia Bank. He brought with him considerable financial-services experience and took on the role of group executive for wealth. Because I did not know Paul personally, this appointment took more time.

During this period I was, of course, highly conscious of the cumulative impact of change. It mattered that executives departing the bank left with as much goodwill as possible. I was fortunate to have the help of my chief financial officer, Steve McKerihan, and my general counsel, Mike Bowan. Both were longstanding employees and went out of their way to support me from the outset. Similarly, I quickly established relationships of trust with other members of the existing team: Greg Bartlett, group executive of the Business and Institutional Bank; John Loebenstein, chief information officer; and Brett Wright, head of human resources.

The team was set – a blend of new and existing skills. Not perfect in every respect, but right for the times. Moving fast, we established a new growth agenda, aligned behind it and began to deliver. As the years progressed, talk of an inevitable takeover receded. The bank was performing too well for any potential acquirer. Changes occurred within the top team over the period, but the foundations were sound and the energy we unleashed was sustained. It was a fun and exciting time marked by high levels of collaboration and

goodwill. I look back on it fondly. The right people for the circumstances were crucial to the bank's performance.

From the outset, a significantly more complex and dynamic set of
issues confronted me in my role as CEO of the Westpac Group.
In selecting me over highly experienced and strongly considered
internal candidates, the board, chaired by Ted Evans, had opted
for a change agent, someone whom they believed could drive a
transformation around customers. That was my mandate and it
became the cornerstone of my agenda. The second major component emerged quickly. As I joined the bank, the global financial
crisis of 2008–09 was already underway. The responsibility to
lead the bank through the extraordinary challenges of this time
became mine. The third substantive agenda item involved first
initiating and then completing our merger with St.George Bank,
a bold move made possible by the crisis. To add to the mix, a further critical area of need emerged: the bank's vulnerable technology
base. Technology outages affecting customers, known as Severity
One outages, were running at a very high average of around 30
per month. A specially commissioned external consultant report
shocked us with the strong language it used to describe the seriousness of our position. Significant investment and new skills were
urgently required. Taken together, this was a formidable agenda.
I would need outstanding people – very many right people in right
roles – to pull it off.

The good news for me was that thanks to David Morgan,
Westpac's previous CEO, the bank was in a strong position both

relatively and absolutely in respect to its credit quality and its risk-management capabilities. In addition, I soon discovered that I had first-class bankers on my team – smart, experienced executives. To assist me in the management of the financial crisis, I particularly drew on the skills and the leadership of our chief financial officer, Phil Coffey. The job he did in coordinating the bank's response was nothing short of outstanding.[6] We were living through a highly volatile and uncertain time. Markets were moving wildly and the pressure was on. Phil worked in a calm and measured way, aligning closely with me and the board. He enlisted the first-class capabilities of colleagues such as Rob Whitfield, Jon Nicholson and Curt Zuber.[7] Working together, we ensured the bases were covered: our funding position, our capital position, our credit portfolios, our response to various stress scenarios, our engagement with regulators and politicians, and our approach to customers. Across the Group, in a non-hierarchical, boundary-less way, we did what was required and emerged strongly. In terms of 'right person, right role', I couldn't have hoped for better.

In my first nine months as CEO of Westpac, I made only the people changes that I believed were absolutely necessary or where gaps needed to be filled. In the environment we were in, stability was paramount and this was the right thing to do. By November 2008, however, I had a solid feel for each member of my team – their strengths, their potential, their ambitions and their alignment with our new customer-centred strategy. I also factored in implications of the merger with St.George and the new business model

---

6   Initiated and chaired by Phil Coffey, the Group established a crisis-management committee codenamed Helix. This cross-divisional, multi-functional body met as often as was necessary, sometimes twice daily, to coordinate and manage our overall response.

7   Rob Whitfield, a longstanding group executive, deeply experienced in risk and in markets; Jon Nicholson, chief strategy officer; Curt Zuber, group treasurer.

we planned to implement. I knew this would provide me with an excellent opportunity for 'right people, right roles' appointments.

On 20 November, 11 days ahead of the merger's effective implementation date, I announced the new structure, together with my executive appointments. In making these selection decisions, I had to juggle a number of elements and seek to achieve the right balance. I did not have a clean sheet of paper – trade-offs were required. My thought process was:

- To ensure stability and continuity, appoint or reappoint key Westpac executives in critical roles for the Group: chief financial officer, chief risk officer, group executives for the Institutional Bank[8], human resources and strategy.

- For the new roles reflecting our merger – in particular, the Retail and Business Banking divisions for Westpac and St.George, and the Product & Operations division – appoint executives who will support and drive the merger objectives, who are likely to collaborate, and who have the energy and passion to motivate and enthuse their newly formed teams.

- For roles where a step-up in capability is required or that necessitate serious remedial work – such as the general counsel and chief information officer roles – appoint trusted, known, commercially savvy 'heavy-hitters' from the outside.

- For the new role of chief transformation officer, appoint the best team member for the job – someone with the skills and experience to drive change and achieve merger and transformation outcomes.

---

8   The Institutional Bank services the needs of the corporate, institutional and government clients of the bank. The division houses specific expertise in financial and debt capital markets.

In making these key people decisions, and in managing the trade-offs involved, I knew that I would not completely achieve the 'right people on the bus, wrong people off the bus' situation. In addition, in the interests of flattening structures and hierarchies, I now had a large team of executives reporting directly to me. Down the track, further decisions would be required to achieve a tighter, more collaborative unit. I felt I could not get there in one step.

To counter the misalignment that emerged from time to time, I placed high demands for teamwork on members of the executive group. I carved out big chunks of time for team engagement on vision, strategy and the operating model. I encouraged individuals to spend one-on-one time together, and to understand each other's personal histories. I worked to establish as much common ground as possible, and as a team we agreed codes of conduct that would guide us when friction emerged. I insisted that solutions be brought to the table, not problems, and that egos be left at the door. In addition, I engaged extensively and directly with the general management cohort of around 100 people and with front-line leaders throughout the company. I wanted to make sure that across the board employees heard the same messages in language that was clear and understandable, not filtered by those who might still be figuring out where the bus was heading and whether they wanted to be on it. This work was systematic and deliberate across the company.

I knew that achieving a cohesive and high-performing Group Executive team would take time, and it did. With the benefit of hindsight, it took longer than it should have. I made some mistakes along the way, including the 'Let me hold off acting now in the hope that things get better' strategy, which seldom works. Towards the end of 2011, I announced an important restructure of the Group's operating model together with new key appointments, and in 2012 we began to hit our straps. A refreshed strategy and a renewed, more closely aligned team resulted in employee engagement reaching its highest recorded level. It became easier to get things done. Belief in what we were doing and trust in each other were strong. We were standing together as a team and were delivering.

When I announced my retirement from the Westpac Group in November 2014, I received an email from one of the bank's most significant investors, Andrew Fleming from Schroders. A few years earlier, Andrew had been invited by our head of investor relations to speak to the team at one of our Group Executive offsites. He spoke frankly and let us know that he was unhappy with our performance and thought we should be achieving more. I knew that part of the issue was that the team was not fully aligned. I suspected that Andrew knew that too. His email at the time of my retirement meant a lot to me. Things had changed, the strength and alignment of the team was now evident. He wrote:

> [You displayed a] genuine desire to build a strong and symbiotic team around you, which is prepared to act collegiately for the benefit of the corporation. The great value of the investor dinners is hearing stories from your executive as to how this informally, as much as formally, occurs, and watching them interact. It's hard to fake teamwork, especially when so many different characters are together. There is a good reason why many corporations don't offer this level of transparency. As Mandela is believed to have said, 'If you talk to a man in a language he understands, that goes to his head. If you talk

to him in his language, that goes to his heart.' It wasn't the case when you started, but in recent years it's clear you enjoyed the respect of your senior executive team; you clearly spoke to their hearts, as well as their heads, and no doubt the collective output is much the better for it.

I deliberately placed this chapter 'Right People, Right Roles' first in the 'Leadership' part of the book. It has been the over-arching leadership lesson of my career. I have found that when you achieve this outcome – right people in right roles – alignment and commitment follow. Everything becomes a lot easier: delivering strong results, tackling transformative agendas, dealing with issues and setbacks. It is also a lot more fun. Throughout my working life in both South Africa and Australia, I have loved spending time with fellow team members. I am extremely proud to say that many have become lifelong friends.

2

PURPOSE, MEANING, AND THE MANAGEMENT OF CULTURE

As a leader, one has the responsibility to help others find meaning and fulfilment in their work. For me, this starts with being very clear on not just what the company is about and needs to achieve, but why it matters – in other words, the company's purpose.

Defining the company's purpose, critically important as it is, is the easy part. Aligning the everyday practices and processes, the decisions and the behaviours, is much harder. What gets the priority: the customer in front of you with a concern, or the next sale?

Are employees who express unhappiness respected and listened to, or are they brushed off and ignored? Is bad news buried, or does it surface quickly? Is 'good enough' seen as good enough?

Culture is sometimes described as 'what happens when no-one is looking'. When no-one is looking, you want to make sure that the company, through all its team members, is living its purpose. This is a leadership job. It is relentless. It requires energy and authenticity coupled with lots and lots of communication, including storytelling. It requires enthusiastically recognising achievement as well as holding individuals to account and taking action when things go wrong. This is true for every business – public and private, big and small. It is true for schools, universities and community organisations of all types. Indeed, it is true for governments and public-service departments.

Be clear on vision and purpose. They will serve as beacons and help drive alignment. Bring them to life with stories and examples. Be consistent. Be authentic. Be transparent. Keep listening and learning.

I devoted myself to this at Westpac, particularly in my latter years there.

The global financial crisis exposed significant weaknesses and failures in the banking system. Understandably, and deservedly, anger against banks and bankers was high. It is obvious now that the industry globally had lost its way, had lost its understanding of its societal role and purpose and, in some cases, bankers had lost their moral compass. Over the period of the crisis and its immediate aftermath, I regularly met with bankers, regulators and politicians at forums such as the World Economic Forum and the International Monetary Conference. Exchanges between these different groups were often tense and, as bankers, we made it worse for ourselves. We argued with regulators, we pushed back on what we saw as excessive regulatory responses, and we tended to exaggerate their cumulative impact.

It was always a relief to return to Australia. Our economy, our banking system, the relationships between regulators, politicians and the industry were much healthier. Our standing with broader society, however, was not good. While banking reputations had improved after the bad days of the late 1990s and early 2000s – the cash-for-comment scandal, the branch-closure program, and the sharp increases in bank fees being features of that period – reputations had plummeted again in the wake of the financial crisis. All of a sudden, Australians were faced with, among other things, 'out-of-cycle'[9] interest-rate rises and a general tightening of credit. Personal financial situations had deteriorated and bank customers questioned the advice or lack of advice they had received. Many felt abandoned and badly treated.

In this challenging 2008–09 period, each bank found its own way of handling a complex set of issues. At Westpac, we took a decision to 'remain open for business', which involved being prepared to meet customers' borrowing needs when most other financial institutions were either restricting access to funding or withdrawing from markets altogether. The effect of this was to put us under earlier pressure than others with regard to the increasingly higher costs of raising funds. We also took a decision to, wherever possible, communicate difficult news directly and personally to our business and corporate customers rather than by letter or email,

---

9   'Out-of-cycle' has become the shorthand description for interest-rate changes that occur at a different time from those announced by the Reserve Bank of Australia, or differ in amount from the Reserve Bank decision.

as was occurring elsewhere in the industry. We encouraged retail customers experiencing financial stress to contact us early and, through Westpac and St.George Assist,[10] we tried to help them.

I recognised however, that what we were doing was not enough. We made mistakes, and many examples of inconsistencies can be found in our treatment of customers. Further, we failed to simply and clearly explain the complex issues we were facing. What Australian customers saw was Australian banks performing relatively well in a country performing relatively well. Why, then, they would ask, are borrowing costs going up so quickly and so steeply? It was not at all obvious how intricately connected Australian banks were to the global financial system. In 2008–09, this global system came very close to collapsing.

In venturing out from time to time to provide explanations for decisions, as bankers we became defensive, trapped in technical terms and jargon. Not surprisingly, we found ourselves defined by media and politicians as 'greedy' and 'out of touch'. The result was a serious and growing loss of trust with customers, and employees becoming increasingly concerned.

The Christmas/New Year period of 2009–10 was a moment of truth for me. In the aftermath of our December interest-rate move, when we raised home-loan rates in a way that caused both shock and anger, I realised I needed to stop and reset. We needed to go back to basics.

Our vision, values and purpose became my starting point. What we stood for, why it mattered, the values we held dear and the behaviours that underpinned them – these elements needed

---

10   Westpac Assist and St.George Assist are discrete operations of the Westpac Group, established to provide assistance to personal and small-business customers in situations of hardship or difficulty.

to be refreshed. They needed to be clear and embraced across our 40 000-person organisation.

In 2010, as a Group Executive team, we commenced this work by conducting workshops around the country with employees of all levels, representing all areas. Everywhere we went, we found huge passion to be involved and to be heard. We formed a team of influential and widely respected general managers to work with us and finalise our vision statement. Getting every word right mattered. Finally, we discussed and agreed on our recommendations with the board.

Our new vision became:

> To be one of the world's great companies,
> *helping* our customers, communities and
> people to prosper and grow.[11]

The emphasis on the word 'helping' is mine and it is quite deliberate. In a nutshell, therein lies our purpose: we exist to provide service to others, to help all of our stakeholder groups to flourish and achieve their goals. I explained this as follows:

- With our people, we seek to provide safe and healthy working environments; we support employees in their careers and in their development, so assisting them to support their families.

- With our customers, be they institutional, corporate, business or retail, our purpose is to build relationships, fully understand needs and to provide service, advice and solutions. Respect, care and thoughtfulness lie at the heart of this.

---

11 Brian Hartzer in 2015 added the word 'service' to the sentence – 'one of the world's great service companies, helping our customers, communities and people to prosper and grow'. This excellent addition set the Group up for the next stage of its journey.

- With communities, help comes in many ways, direct and indirect. It includes proactive engagement and assistance in times of special need such as a natural disaster, as well as month in, month out support of local initiatives. It includes running a bank well, paying our taxes, and providing a steady stream of dividends to our investors.
- With regard to shareholders, fulfilling this vision properly will result in Westpac enduring into the future in a sustainable way. One of the world's great companies – exactly what long-term shareholders are looking for.

Every single employee in the company is able to contribute to this purpose, whatever his or her role. Each one can reflect at the end of a day on 'How did I help today, who did I help today, and what might I seek to do tomorrow?'

A company's values should, of course, stand the test of time. Based on the input from our employees and broader management team, we decided to add a new one: courage. The banking world requires boldness, innovation and a preparedness to speak up and challenge. The full set of values are:

Integrity, Achievement, Delighting Customers,
Courage, One Team

The really important work for the leaders of Westpac now began: making sure that what were essentially words on paper translated into meaning and relevance across the organisation; making sure that the words became much more than words – that they were properly reflected in the company's processes, policies, practices and behaviours, making sure that all our stakeholders would experience the difference.

We started this process with communication, using every possible medium. Each Group Executive team member and general manager stepped up to deliver consistent, energy-filled communications, bringing the company's vision and values to life. Personally I loved this part of my job. At every opportunity, internally and externally, I would discuss what we stood for as a bank and why it mattered. I put a high value on getting the language, tone and mood of the communication just right, and used stories to amplify the messages and make them tangible. I drew links between behaviours and performance, outlined expectations and set high standards. Of course, I realised that in setting the bar high for our 40 000-person team, I was raising the bar even higher for myself. I would be measured not by what I said, but by what I did: how visibly and consistently did I live the values? Nothing less than complete authenticity would do.

As a bit of fun, really, I sometimes spoke of 'the elevator pitch', the idea being that if you ('you' being a Westpac employee) and I got into the elevator on the ground floor, I would ask you to call out, in the short period of our journey, the essence of our vision or name our values. You wouldn't need to get it word perfect, of course – just show you had a fundamental grasp of it. Every now and then, an excited team member sharing the elevator with me would say, 'Can we do it? Can we do the elevator pitch?' Anyone joining us along the way would step in to find at least two people enthusiastically talking about *Helping*, about *Integrity, Achievement, Delighting Customers, Courage* and *One Team.*

One Friday afternoon, when Allan had come to meet me, we

were joined in the elevator on the way to the lobby by a young executive. Allan, who knew about 'the elevator pitch' and who has a fun sense of humour, proceeded to ask the unsuspecting fellow traveller: 'I wonder if you could tell me Westpac's four values?' She smiled, looked at me and then at him, and said, 'Well, actually, we have five.'

Internally, we referred to this work on communication and behaviours, on storytelling and role-modelling, as 'soft-wiring'. 'Hard-wiring'[12] related to the 'change work' that was required on policies, processes and practices to ensure that they were consistent with the company's vision and values. Every element of what we did needed to be reassessed. In the HR world, for example, this included recruitment and selection of employees, induction, training and development, performance management and remuneration. Major changes included:

- hiring for attitude and values alignment first, before assessing for technical requirements;
- company-wide workshops on behaviours;
- case studies built into training programs;
- balanced scorecards reflecting the focus on customers, employees and strategy implementation. My own scorecard, which cascaded through the organisation, had a 50 per cent weighting on financial and risk management metrics and 50 per cent on these other elements;
- for frontline sales and service employees, scorecards were changed to reflect the requirement to fully understand customer needs. We introduced the idea of 'great

12 I love the terms 'hard-wiring' and 'soft-wiring' and have found them very useful in driving a number of change initiatives. They were used as a throwaway line by one of the Group Executive team members, Peter Hanlon, at a culture offsite in late 2009. I immediately seized on them, and they became part of our apparatus for driving change.

conversations'[13] and instead of product per customer metrics, we started to measure what we called 'My Bank' customers;[14] [15]

- throughout the company, an explicit assessment of behaviour became a key component of each team member's performance evaluation – any individual who rated poorly faced consequences in terms of remuneration and career prospects;
- being really clear on what happens in the case of misconduct;
- 360-degree evaluations for senior teams.

Sales and marketing practices as well as product policies and processes required refreshing, too. In a nutshell, alignment with our vision and values meant being clear and transparent with customers, properly understanding their needs and doing the right thing. We utilised customer-centred design techniques and a checklist approach when developing or launching new products. Were we following through on what we said? We encouraged debate, and designated a team member with the specific role of representing the customer at the discussion. We held line managers accountable for their decisions. When things went wrong, and breaches or mistakes occurred, we encouraged and rewarded fast feedback and fast action. We all knew it was best to find our own mistakes rather than have them turn up in an audit or regulatory review.

---

13 'Great conversations' are properly structured conversations focused on customer needs and providing pathways to help.

14 'My Bank' customers have their active, in-use transaction accounts with us; in addition we meet at least two of their other financial needs, for example, their savings, protection or long-term borrowing needs.

15 Brian Hartzer and his executive team have taken this work to the next level. For example, all product-related incentives for tellers and personal bankers have been removed.

We strengthened our compliance protocols, emphasising first-line responsibilities. We trusted and then we verified.

What I am describing here is the management of culture, something that needs to be high on the agenda for all organisations, big or small, public or private. The example I use here – that of banking – is particularly effective in bringing to the fore just how critical it is to have a sound ethically-based culture.

As discussed, all around the world – including in Australia – banks face serious reputational challenges, and the trust gap has grown. Poor cultures are at the heart of this. While regulators, supervisors and politicians play their parts in building a much safer, more resilient banking system, the responsibility for fixing the culture of an organisation lies with its board and management. I feel very strongly about this. Culture cannot be regulated. It differs from bank to bank, which is healthy and as it should be. Supervisors have the important and value-adding role of challenging boards and management on how they understand, measure and manage culture. They can also compare and contrast across organisations and share best practice, so raising the bar for all. In the event of serious breaches, or misconduct, they have the tools to penalise banks and individuals within banks.

It is evident that banks are in different stages in their journey of managing culture. As a member of the Group of Thirty (G30), I contributed to the July 2015 report entitled 'Banking Conduct and Culture: A Call for Sustained and Comprehensive Reform'.[16] More than 70 bank leaders in 16 countries were interviewed, and

---

16   The G30 report was produced by a committee co-chaired by Roger W. Ferguson, Jr., former vice chairman, Board of Governors of the US Federal Reserve System, and William R. Rhodes, president and CEO, William R. Rhodes Global Advisors. It is essentially a call to action and outlines detailed and practical recommendations for banks and regulators. A follow-up review is expected in 2018.

the report comes to the conclusion that while most banks have the 'what to aspire to' in place, they are still largely failing in implementation. Some approach cultural reform in a piecemeal fashion, while others are reactive and defensive. As the report outlines, what is required is a fundamental shift in mindset and a comprehensive approach.

I know from experience that this is hard work and that it is never-ending. It can often feel like one step forward and several back. Each new incident of poor behaviour or wrongdoing undermines the progress that has been made, reinforces the negative sentiment towards the industry, and damages public trust. Wrongdoing at one bank carries the risk of contagion to others. Further, banks are easy public targets, and in the current fraught political environment, they form part of the punch and counterpunch between political parties. This is certainly the case in Australia. A series of reputational scandals across the industry has seen a ratcheting-up of negativity and of populism, with sustained calls for a royal commission into banks.

It is imperative in this rather dispiriting environment for bank leadership to be visible, to publicly engage on the issues and to be seen to be taking action. My reflections are:

- The internal work on purpose, meaning and the management of culture is even more important. Getting one's own house in order is the first priority. Systematically setting about ensuring that customers are placed ahead of profits, that business practices are ethical and transparent, that policies and processes are in place to encourage and reward good conduct and to penalise bad behaviour, and that robust listening and feedback mechanisms, including whistleblowing, have been institutionalised – this work is critical and never-ending. Getting it right will serve as a source of major competitive advantage.

- As an industry, identify the main 'pain points' with customers and seek to remedy them. In Australia, incentive structures that result in actual or perceived conflicts of interest are one such pain point. The standards and monitoring of financial advice are another. Set tough industry-led codes of behaviour and install a transparent and independent process for review and oversight.

- Adopt a proactive approach with regulators, going well beyond what is required in terms of compliance. Not only is this likely to result in more favourable outcomes, but it is also a litmus test for the transparency and openness of the culture.

- Be prepared to step up publicly and apologise when necessary. Apologies need to be timely and genuine, be transparent, and show empathy and humility. They need to encompass the redressing of wrongs. It is important to use an active voice: 'I apologise', 'I take responsibility'. Saying 'We acknowledge that errors have been made' just will not do.

- Collectively and individually, CEOs and chairpersons need, on a regular basis, to openly discuss the critical role of banks in society, to talk through the difficult balancing act required among various stakeholder groups, and to properly and in an understandable way explain tough decisions that have been made or need to be made. Use both rational and emotional arguments. 'Strong banks support a financially strong economy' is a rational argument. 'Strong banks are deeply connected to the community: they provide jobs, enable businesses to grow and individuals to save for their homes or their retirement' is communicating on a more emotional level, particularly when the words are delivered in plain language and are backed up with real-life stories. My own efforts in this area were episodic and insufficient. They were not always addressed to the right audiences. The platforms I used tended to be those of traditional mainstream media. I also frequently adopted the strategy of seeking to be a small target. This worked to some extent in earlier years; it is no longer the right approach. The noise level is high, the outrage is real, and bankers keeping their heads down creates a vacuum that others will fill.

- Fully utilise social media platforms to discuss the issues – they can help in building understanding and advocacy. Encourage employees, suppliers and community partners to get involved. As an example, GE Voices, the website launched by Jeff Immelt, chairman and CEO of General Electric, does just this and has proved extremely powerful in articulating, through the voices of employees and suppliers, what the company stands for, and how it goes about its business, playing its part in building a stronger economy and society.

- Finally, never let up. Whatever your company or business, be clear on its purpose. Not just what you do, but why it matters. As leader, fiercely guard against impatience, frustration, complacency or arrogance. Communicate, communicate, communicate. Refresh the messages.

Tell stories to bring your values to life. Show you are serious. Be visible. Be authentic. Set high standards and hold yourself and the organisation to account.

This work, the work of shaping and managing culture, is leadership work. It matters a lot, perhaps more than anything.

3

PASSION FOR
CUSTOMERS

January 14, 1980. My first day in banking. My position: a teller in the Simmonds Street branch, Johannesburg, of the South African Permanent Building Society.

Allan and I lived in a high-rise apartment in Berea, an inner-city neighbourhood of Johannesburg. I walked to work each morning, a good 30-minute walk, and, in stark contrast to my previous six months as a teacher, I looked forward to every day. Working within a team, serving customers, learning new things – I loved it.

I hadn't expected to love it. Going into banking was a stop-gap job for me while I figured out what I really wanted to do. For example, I had simultaneously signed up for a course at UNISA (the University of South Africa) in Ancient Greek. Allan was in his second year of medicine at the University of the Witwatersrand, so full-time study was not an option for me. I needed a job. With some help from my father, I secured an entry-level position in banking.

Early on, I learned three things. One, I loved the engagement with customers – doing my best to serve them and give them a good experience. Two, as a teller, you were perceived to be on the bottom rung of the ladder. Yet with only the most rudimentary level of training, essentially learning 'as you go', you were entrusted to look after what I saw as the bank's most important asset: its customers. Three, career progression involved moving into the back office away from customers, to departments such as 'Term Deposit Renewal', 'Overdrafts', 'Accounting' and 'Credit'. Those jobs came with more money, more prestige, more training and more clout. Even as a very junior, new person in banking, this seemed wrong to me. If I am ever in management, I thought, I will do it differently. A bank needs to be totally customer-centric. When the chance to 'do it differently' arose, I found that transforming a business around its customers is not a simple thing to do.

In each of my last three major roles in banking – Group Executive, Customer Service Division for the Commonwealth Bank; CEO, St.George Bank; and CEO, Westpac – putting customers at the centre was key to the strategy.[17]

---

17 'Putting customers at the centre' is a phrase that is increasingly used by organisations to describe their strategies, and runs the risk of becoming an empty slogan. For me, a strategy that authentically puts customers at the centre of the business starts and ends with the customer in mind. It requires all parts of the organisation to pull together, break down barriers and innovate, in order to deliver a great experience. Its core tenet is simply: do the right thing for the customer.

Implementation was, for the most part, easiest at St.George, with its historical service culture and its natural orientation to looking after customers. The major challenge within that organisation was the need to introduce a more proactive model of engagement with customers, and to do this in a way that front-line employees would accept. I understood how critical it was to 'work with the grain' of the culture, celebrating the strengths that were there and extending them further. We needed to explain that when done correctly, sales and service go hand in hand. In order to deliver really good service to customers, you need to understand their needs and circumstances and then provide advice and potential solutions. You have to be prepared to have a conversation. And so the culture shift towards more proactivity and deeper engagement with customers began. We made sure that everyone across the company was included. 'If you are not yourself serving a customer, you are serving someone who is' became a philosophy for us.

Putting real focus and weight on those in the very front line, who were serving customers directly, involved significant culture change. As an executive team, we led by example. We spent time 'in the field', 'adopting' branches and business-banking centres; we set up a 'Listening Post' in the call centres in Kogarah and Parramatta; and we directed that all managers in head office or operational roles were required to spend a minimum of four hours in the front line each month. They could learn to be tellers and help out on a Saturday morning, they could provide general service and support to the branch manager and his or her team, or spend time at the Listening Post. It was exciting to see how eyes opened, how product managers and technology leaders better understood the impact of their decisions on the customer experience, and how enthusiastic and innovative they became.

With managers in the front line, as well as relevant head office executives, we also initiated a 'Call five customers a week' program. I would block out my Friday afternoons and set about my personal calling program. It was easy to find customers to call – new customers to the bank, customers who had written to me directly with a complaint, longstanding customers who were celebrating an event or anniversary. Not surprisingly, I learned a lot through these calls. And also not surprisingly, I was often able to win more business. Usually, the only people surprised were the customers themselves. I would sometimes have to devote the opening minutes of the call to convincing the customer that it was actually me. On one occasion, buddying with a service representative in our Kogarah call centre, a customer asked, 'Your CEO is that bird from South Africa, isn't she?' It was great fun to connect directly with the customer and say, 'Hello, yes, you are speaking to her. How are you?'

All of this, however, served as practice for my Westpac job. I was determined to take this strategy of putting customers at the centre even further, to fully embed it across the organisation. It was the mandate I had been assigned by chairman Ted Evans and the Westpac board. I knew it would not be easy and would take time. I did not contemplate dealing with a financial crisis and a major merger over the same period.

February 1, 2008, was my first day in the office. Following on from my St.George practice of regularly sending personal emails to the whole team, I set about my first Westpac email. It was a very simple and straightforward message, introducing myself, saying how thrilled and honoured I was to be the new CEO, and sharing

things that I deeply care about: a passion for people and for delighting customers. The team around me were very nervous. A CEO
writing her own message to staff was not normal. What might she
say? We should be doing it for her, to get the tone and style right.
So I handed my draft email over for review and saw the relief on
their faces as they came back to me. Yes, this will be fine. Only one
word had been changed: 'delighted' became 'satisfied'.

'Having engaged, committed staff who enjoy what they do and
having *delighted* customers go hand in hand' had become '. . . having
satisfied customers go hand in hand'.

Very interesting, I thought. Why the change? And I was given
my first Westpac lesson: 'Gail, Westpac is a major bank. We don't
do "delight".' Aha, let the revolution begin.[18] The full email read as
follows:

> **Friday 1 February 2008**
> Before I say anything else, I would like to say how delighted I am
> to officially be a member of the Westpac team. 17 August 2007 –
> the day of my appointment – seems like a very long time ago, and
> in recent weeks I have been counting down the days! I feel **very**
> honoured and privileged to be here.
>
> Of course, I fully recognise that I have very big shoes to fill.
> David Morgan has done an outstanding job as CEO of Westpac
> over the past 9 years and he leaves a strong legacy. I would like
> to personally thank him for his support and for his assistance in
> facilitating a strong transition.
>
> As you might expect, I will be doing a lot of listening and
> learning over the next couple of months. I intend to get out
> and about as much as possible – meeting our people and our
> customers. I am particularly keen to understand the extent to
> which we are truly meeting our customers' needs, and what more

---

18   In telling this story at People Leader Forums, which were held twice each year at major centres
      around Australia, I sometimes further expanded on why the word 'satisfaction' didn't do the
      trick. I would draw on my Latin background and explain the derivation of the word. *Satis* means
      'enough', and 'faction' comes from *facio*, meaning 'to make' or 'to do'. So 'doing enough' – that's
      not what it's about, I would say.

we need to do (or stop doing) to achieve this in a consistent way. In addition, I would love to hear what you think needs to be done to make it easier for our people to serve our customers. As some of you may already be aware, I am deeply and genuinely passionate about both our people and our customers. Of course, having engaged, committed staff who enjoy what they do and having delighted customers go hand in hand.

Please do not hesitate to let me know your thoughts and ideas on these topics. There will be a number of ways to reach me; one of the easiest will be simply to email me directly. I would love to hear from you.

In closing, thank you for your support and your welcome. I am excited to be here and I look forward to working with you all in the months and years ahead.

Email Gail directly – gailkelly@westpac.com.au[19]

In February and March, while the early winds of the financial crisis swirled around us, and the thinking and preparation for a potential merger with St. George began to get underway, I launched a formal program of work to design a new customer-centred strategy. My aim was to achieve sign-off at the board strategy meeting being held in July. To lead this work I chose Jason Yetton who, on my arrival, had been identified as the highest-performing, highest-potential general manager in the Group. Coming from BT, the Group's wealth management business, Jason had a naturally strong empathy for and commitment to customers. It would be fair to say that he was not certain this was a good next move for him. Running a transformational strategy program is risky at the best of times, and this one involved a new CEO.

Jason and I met one Saturday morning in my office, where I expanded on my vision of change. I discussed the lessons I had

---

19   In many of my emails written over the years, I included a personal story or set of remarks involving my family – for example, the challenges of having three 17-year-olds on their L-plates, or the tears and joy associated with Year 12 examinations. Interestingly, years later, this is what people remember and recount back to me.

learned in my career in driving a customer-centric strategy, and how we would build on these lessons but push harder and further. Jason looked at me and said, 'If you are really serious about this, I am in.' We shook hands on it.

Like all good programs, we gave this one a name: Twenty17. April 8, 2017, was to be the bank's 200th anniversary – an extraordinary achievement and one to celebrate. Twenty17 would therefore set out to describe, in clear and aspirational terms, what we wanted for our bank on this important milestone – what we would like our customers, our shareholders, our employees and members of the broader community to say about us. What were our financial and non-financial goals to be? The nine-year time horizon gave us the freedom to be bold.

The program then set out to develop the framework for implementation, identifying the key pillars required to underpin the change.

As was typical for a major bank, Westpac was a product-focused organisation. The bank's balance sheet resided with product managers who were responsible for pricing and volume decisions. They had the power to determine priorities and to direct frontline sales and service employees. The consequences of this organisational model were that the best skills resided in product and by far the lion's share of investment occurred here. Sales and service distribution teams had over the years been starved of investment, and those employees were undervalued and not empowered.

My first official visit to a Westpac branch took place within a week of commencing. I was with Peter Hanlon, the group executive for business banking, visiting one of his centres in the western suburbs of Sydney. On the spur of the moment, we decided to pop in to the local branch as well. It was a very pleasant visit with a rather nervous young branch manager. I asked him how many customers he looked after in his branch and the size of the lending and deposit balances he managed. For a moment, he looked bewildered. Was this something he should know? Peter explained to me that this information was not held at branch level and assured the young man that none of his colleagues would know either. I asked what the key business measures for the branch were, and he pointed to the number of sales achieved – for example, the number of new accounts opened. Major success drivers such as growth in customer numbers, growth of overall balances, depth of relationship and customers' likeliness to recommend, were not being tracked at this level.

I asked the branch manager to introduce me to his team and I met his welcoming tellers and customer-service officers. What about the home finance manager, the financial planner and the business banker in the upstairs offices? 'No,' the branch manager said, 'they do not report to me – they report directly to their respective product areas in head office.' He assured me that they had a standing invitation to attend his weekly meetings.

In approaching the branch, I had noticed that the ATM outside was grubby, with a pile of rubbish heaped up in front. I asked him about this. 'Oh,' he said, 'yes, of course. I will see that it is cleaned up. It is not something we normally do. The property team is responsible for ATMs.'

I learned a lot in that visit. Under our Twenty17 customer-centred strategy, big shifts would be required.

First step in the implementation of the newly signed-off strategy was bringing into being a new structure. By this stage, we were well underway with the planning for our merger with St.George and we took this into account in our design. In effect, we turned the organisation on its head. Frontline distribution businesses – the businesses that directly engage with customers – became *the* businesses, with balance-sheet and profit-and-loss accountability. Previously, product, operations and head-office functions had made the key decisions of 'what, when, where'. Under the new model, their role became one of partnering and supporting, rather than directing. Final accountability for the customer experience and for bottom-line performance would sit with those businesses in the very front line.

Particularly in the Westpac brand, a huge transformation and skills build was required. Peter became our group executive for Westpac Retail & Business Banking (WRBB), with Jason his general manager for Retail. They set about the implementation of the strategy with an energy and passion that surprised even me. Every now and then, I or Phil Coffey, our CFO, would lift up our heads and say, 'You've done what? Already?' – even, 'Are you sure?'

And so, over a period of several years, with an upfront investment of $166 million, a revolution occurred in Westpac's retail business. The bank manager was back. The switch in title from branch manager to bank manager was quite deliberate. We recalled the days when bank managers were deeply respected and important figures in their local communities. They had the authority and skills to make decisions for customers, and were empowered to run their branches like their own businesses. We set out to establish the customer experience of that model.

This was not just a matter of renaming existing branch managers. The newly created bank manager role was considerably more senior. Over 650 new appointments were made, drawn from current regional managers, commercial managers, financial advisers and product managers; carefully selected external appointments occurred too, several of whom were from outside the industry. We looked for men and women, achieving an overall 50:50 split, from the local community in which the branch was situated. The level of pay was on average 30 per cent higher than that previously earned by branch managers, and well above industry levels.

This was a revolution in the bank. The branch manager had been at the end of the chain, being directed and told what to do; the bank manager was at the front of the process, empowered to look after the customer. She was able to direct others in operational and head-office areas to assist her in expeditiously solving problems and meeting needs. She was directly involved in determining the mix of skills required in her branch. She could decide what time the branch would open and close, including over the weekend. She could set the priorities for the team in line with the requirements of her business plan, and she had some dollars to spend in local marketing. She even had a degree of discretion in pricing.

At the same time we set about branch refurbishments, redesigns and relocations. Frontline technology was overhauled to improve stability and reliability, and new teller and customer-information systems were implemented. With a considerable degree of difficulty, we devolved balance-sheet and profit-and-loss statements to the branch and instituted new revenue measures. Also with some difficulty, we introduced a branch-level net promoter score (NPS) system to track customer feedback and likeliness to recommend at the local level. On my branch visits, the NPS was the very first thing the team wanted to share with me: the most recent score, how it was trending, what customers were saying, and what actions the team were taking.[20]

Frontline staff exuded passion for customers. It was infectious across the organisation. The customer came first, and the strategy worked. Over a six-year period from 2009 to 2015, WRBB achieved phenomenal outcomes. Cash earnings increased from $1.9 billion to $2.8 billion, while the number of customers, which was 4.9 million in 2009, increased to 6.5 million. Most significantly of all, employee engagement increased from what was an already high 81 per cent to a remarkable 93 per cent.

As a direct consequence of our focus on customers and customer service, we introduced new protocols with regard to product, pricing and marketing decisions. Executives were required to explicitly address the issues of 'Is this the right thing to do?' and 'Are the changes transparent and understandable?' We also began to ask to what extent customers had been engaged and consulted. Starting in our wealth division, BT, we implemented a new customer-centred design methodology that involved not only obtaining customer feedback and advice but also observing customers 'in the field', looking at what they actually did.

An early example of where we applied this approach was in the area of superannuation. With its compulsory contribution model, Australia has the fifth-largest pension pool globally. By mid-2015, superfund assets stood at $2 trillion, and they are projected to grow to $9.5 trillion by 2035. The fact was, however, that Australians had

---

20 We measured NPS monthly at branch level. In call centres, daily feedback was received.

typically not engaged with their superannuation. Understanding was poor and in many cases, as employees moved jobs, their superannuation was located in more than one place. If you asked an Australian how much they owed on their home loan, you would get an answer that was about right, but ask how much they had in their super and the most likely answer would be 'I don't know'. Ask how super actually works and many would say: 'It's all a bit of a mystery to me.'

As Westpac thought about this market, the challenges were clear. The BT team, led by Rob Coombe, decided to engage with customers and ask them what they wanted. We received a consistent set of answers:

- 'Please make super understandable.'
- 'Make it easy to access, just as our savings and home loans are easy to access.'
- 'Ensure that it is cost effective, with a simple, transparent fee structure.'
- 'Make it something we can take with us as we move from one employer to another.'
- 'Make the investment profile something we can easily adjust as changes occur in our life circumstances.'

Out of these customer-led specifications emerged Westpac's 'Super for Life' – a very simple, easy-to-set-up, cost-effective and transparent super product that could be opened in a branch, through a call centre or online, and could be seen and tracked just as the customer could see and monitor his or her savings account. As its title suggests, it is transportable through life, regardless of where the customer is employed.

This product was transformational in the Australian super land-scape. The fact that we could provide general information on the product through the branch network was transformational, too. Tellers and customer-service officers had typically stayed well away from conversations with customers about super – it was too complex an area. This product, however, was simple and easy to understand. Customer-service officers themselves liked the product and so were happy to outline its features and, where appropriate, provide referrals for further advice.

One of the key metrics in our Westpac Local model became 'Customers who also have a wealth product with us'. From a low base, the percentage steadily increased to stand at 20 per cent by 2015, recognised as a standout result both locally and globally. The linkage of banking and wealth for our customers became a competitive advantage for the Group and critical to building deeper relationships that would last. It started with a product design process that listened to customers' issues, understood what they were looking for, and set out to meet the need.

A further example of implementing change based on an assessment of 'Is this the right thing for customers?' involved finally tackling the matter of exception fees. These widely disliked fees, which often appeared unexpectedly, applied to activities such as exceeding a limit on your credit card, a late payment, or over-drawing your personal or business account. Like every other large financial institution, we had fees in place for these situations, some as high as $45 per incident. Banking fees are generally unwelcome but these in particular were roundly criticised by consumer groups for being too high and not transparent enough. Our bank had over the years evaluated the situation but backed off material change.

In August 2009, we finally acted. We cut all exception fees on credit cards and on personal and business accounts to $9. We applied this across all our brands in both Australia and New Zealand. We were disappointed that National Australia Bank had beaten us to the punch the previous week by abolishing their overdrawn-account fees on personal accounts, but our decision was far more comprehensive, affecting many more customers and many more accounts.

At the same time, we introduced new initiatives that would assist customers to avoid the requirement for a fee at all – for example, text messaging customers to let them know when they were close to their credit limits and giving them time to address the matter. The overall financial impact of this set of decisions was around $300 million. What delighted me most was the extremely positive internal response. The board asked us why it had taken so long, and executives and employees said, 'Yes, this is the right thing to do – for customers, for our communities and for our shareholders. This is about being sustainable.'

The next steps in our customer-centred strategy occurred in 2012. Five years away from our bicentennial, we decided that a refresh was necessary. New digital technologies, including mobile, big data, social media and cloud computing were coming into their own. It was around this time that I asked Brian Hartzer to join the Group in the new position of CEO, Australian Financial Services. Brian brought with him a deep understanding of the power of these technologies, and innovative ideas on how to put them to work to give customers a great service experience.

Our new program, 2017+, was underpinned by three simple elements: 'Know Me', 'Empower Me' and 'BankWow'. As a team, we recognised that banking needed to be made a lot easier and more intuitive for customers; that customers expected us to know them and to deliver personalised solutions and advice; that customers wanted to be able to seamlessly navigate our various channels and engage with us when and how they chose; that they were looking for a great experience. As a team, we knew that to deliver on this promise work needed to be done differently: smaller projects, shorter timeframes, multidisciplinary teams with decision powers, iterating and reiterating, testing and learning, designing and innovating from the customer perspective. We launched an innovation hub in Kogarah called 'The Hive' and set up, and freed up, an internal team known as the MAD[21] team. We fundamentally redesigned a number of key product processes – for example, George Frazis's[22] '60-minute mortgage', which became a welcome new standard for home-loan approvals. We strengthened our data analytics team, leveraging a wide set of technologies, digital and analog, quantitative and qualitative, to assist us in gaining actionable insights. We also took the step of setting up and investing in a new venture capital fund, Reinventure, in order to gain insights into the emerging fintech (financial technology) business model, assessing what we could apply internally and learning how to execute at speed.

In November 2014, Brian was appointed the next CEO of Westpac, taking up the position in February 2015. His strategy is one of a Service Revolution. It is exciting to see the next chapter unfold. The passion for customers is not only continuing – it is ratcheting up in intensity and focus.

---

21   MAD stands for Mobile Application Development.
22   George Frazis joined Westpac in 2009 as CEO, Westpac New Zealand. Several of the innovations he drove in that market were later transported to Australia when he became CEO of St.George in 2012.

I will confess that I often worried, especially in the early years of my Westpac career, that speaking so much and so passionately about customers would have the 'serious-minded' people of banking – long-time senior executives, analysts, investment bankers, fund managers – wanting to roll their eyes. And I know that sometimes that happened. What often gets missed, however, is that there is a very direct link between employees who are engaged and customers having great experiences. There is a very direct link between customers having great experiences and superior shareholder results over time. Customers who feel valued stay with the bank, do more business with the bank, and refer others.

This is a simple philosophy, and it works. It is true in banking. It is true in all businesses. Passion for customers is what it takes.

4

LEAD WITH COURAGE

Today's world is one of extraordinary change and uncertainty. Leaders are confronted with increasingly complex and interconnected issues. With the advent of social media and the 24-hour news cycle, scrutiny of leaders' actions and behaviours has never been higher. Against this backdrop, it has become even more important to lead with courage, to be able to articulate a bold vision and execute on it fearlessly, to persevere when the pressure is on, to stand firm under fire from the naysayers, and to persist in what you believe is right. This is not easy, especially when you are in the midst of it.

I do not regard myself as being particularly courageous. As discussed in the final chapter of Part I of this book, I have repeatedly had to dig deep and to back myself. Being disciplined, hardworking and fiercely determined has helped. I am also drawn to Virgil's phrase *Audentes fortuna iuvat* – Fortune favours the ones who dare.

My seven years as CEO of Westpac was certainly the most challenging period of my career – the first five years in particular. As discussed in the 'Right People, Right Roles' chapter, my agenda essentially had four prongs:

- leading the company through the extraordinary times of the global financial crisis;
- undertaking Australia's largest financial services merger;
- designing and driving the transformational customer-centred strategy; and
- fixing our vulnerable technology base and establishing the foundation for the digital revolution.[23]

The piece of the agenda that drew most on my personal courage was that of the St.George merger. Dealing with the financial crisis was not discretionary – the St.George merger was. People sometimes ask me whether I came across to Westpac with the explicit intention, or even direction, to facilitate a merger with St.George. The answer is no.

What enabled the opportunity to come onto the table in early 2008 and be workable was the disruption to global funding markets.

---

23   To tackle this sizeable technology issue, we established, under board sponsorship, a five-year, $2 billion strategic investment program known as SIPs. Bob McKinnon and John Arthur were outstanding in their leadership of what proved to be a hugely ambitious and critically important program of work.

All Australian banks were impacted, but smaller banks with a single 'A' rating or lower were hit hardest. Equity markets reflected these vulnerabilities and share prices fell. Long-held files of desirable targets in the mergers and acquisitions (M&A) departments of major banks were dusted off and fresh assessments were made. And of the four major banks, only two had the firepower to pursue large in-market mergers: Westpac and the Commonwealth Bank.

On 4 February 2008, my second day in office, I met with Jon Nicholson, our chief strategy officer, and Harvey Carter, head of M&A. They came armed with a high-level analysis of all potential targets – and with the expectation of being sent away. Any new CEO is going to want time, they reasoned. Instead, I looked at the set and pointed to the biggest option available. 'St.George Bank – that's the one,' I said.

Coming directly from St.George, I knew what a good fit a Westpac–St.George merger would be. I had spent years at St.George focusing on its defence strategy. We had had our own detailed files, one for each of the potential acquirers. St.George was an attractive target. Its heartland lay in New South Wales and its core business was consumer and business banking. Its wealth-management subsidiary, Asgard, was primarily a platform for wealth administration, supporting and serving a high-quality network of independent financial advisers. Thanks to a prior acquisition, St.George also owned Bank of South Australia (BankSA), a bank actively supported by one in three South Australians. Overall, St.George looked after three million customers and held around $120 billion in lending balances, $80 billion in deposits and $40 billion in funds under management/administration. Merging St.George with Westpac would move the Westpac Group to a strong No.1 or No.2 position in home lending, retail deposits, business banking and wealth management markets.

In addition, a key strength that St.George would bring was its culture and its reputation for serving customers. No doubt drawing on its building society roots, St.George was well known for its warmth, friendliness and close links to the community. Happy Dragon, the bank's rather quirky mascot who couldn't help bringing a smile to your face, was a favourite at local events and loved by employees. As reflected in the well-known advertisement 'I'm a banker . . . I'm with St.George',[24] the organisation was seen as different from the major banks – more connected and more caring. It was clear to me that a merger with St.George would assist in our strategy of transformation around customers within Westpac. I believed it would help accelerate the process of change.

Still, notwithstanding everything that would be positive about a merger between the companies, it would be a big call. It would be a particularly big call for me, as the brand-new CEO of Westpac. I was fully aware that it also carried significant personal risk. Announcing the transaction and then failing to bring it home would be reputationally problematic for me; much worse would be concluding the transaction and then executing on it poorly, so exposing Westpac and its investors to substantial downside risk.

In my overall judgement, however, the opportunity outweighed the risks. A Westpac–St.George merger would be transformative for the bank. I had a clear vision of what was required in respect to integration, and of how to set about ensuring long-term value. And

---

24   The television advertisement depicts an everyday Australian barbecue scene in the backyard around the pool. 'What do you do for a living, David?' is the question. 'Me? I'm a banker' is the response. Everything stops – the conversation around the table, the kids playing in the pool, even the dog drinking from his bowl. After a long pause, David comes back with an explanatory 'I'm with St.George', and everybody relaxes, smiling and laughing, and resumes their activities. The take-home message: that's okay then – St.George is different.

so I drew on my courage and acted decisively. The Westpac team was mobilised. We updated the work on all potential targets and engaged in a full and open discussion with the board. The analysis was unequivocal: St.George Bank was the 'swing asset' in Australia and whoever acquired it would become larger, stronger and competitively better positioned.

We were fully aware that this was a 'Bet the Bank' decision. Being around one-third the size of Westpac, St.George did not fit into the category of a small 'bolt-on' acquisition. A significant number of steps and approvals were required. First and foremost, we needed to win the support of the St.George Bank board – a friendly transaction was the only way an in-market merger could work. In addition, the permission of Australia's federal treasurer was necessary, as well as the approval of the Australian Competition and Consumer Commission (ACCC). The St.George shareholders would have the final say. As we mapped out our plan, we were acutely aware that all of this would be taking place against the backdrop of the evolving financial crisis and a deteriorating economic environment.

On 12 May 2008, 102 days after my start date as Westpac CEO, we announced the merger deal with St.George Bank. Chairman-to-chairman talks over the previous weekend had been successful. The announcement of this $18.6 billion transaction took the market by surprise, and our foyer in Westpac Place was filled with journalists, cameras and television crews. 'Banks agree on a mega-merger' was a typical newspaper headline. Part of the interest was just how quickly and comprehensively we had put the transaction together and reached agreement. Bold leadership from a number of players, not least our wise, thoughtful chairman, Ted Evans, had achieved this outcome.

My newness as CEO of Westpac, coupled with my previous role as CEO of St.George, brought particular requirements for me in initiating and managing the transaction.[25] I needed strong and deeply experienced Westpac leaders alongside me – individuals who had credibility with executive colleagues and the board, independent thinkers with good judgement and thorough understanding of financial markets. I needed team members who could effectively mobilise others. Most important of all, I needed leaders around me I could trust. In Rob Whitfield, Phil Coffey and Jon Nicholson, the three most senior players, I got all this.

As lead executive I chose Rob, a banker who described himself the first time I met him as having 'little red Ws in his bloodstream'. This was not surprising as Rob's father, John, had served the bank for 40 years. Rob himself had over 20 years notched up, including important periods as treasurer and chief risk officer for the Group. At our very first meeting, he and I had connected. On a handshake, we said that we were in this together. And so when it came to the St.George merger, it was to him I turned. Rob built a first-rate team and brought impressive intellectual rigour and discipline to the program. He moved at pace, tackling difficult issues head-on and building alignment across the organisation. The two of us had many a robust conversation on the issues at stake and the best negotiating approach. Rob knew better than anyone the realities of the global markets we were confronting. I recall an important conversation with him shortly after the collapse of Lehman Brothers. We discussed the enormous risks the industry was facing. We discussed our position, the uncertainties, the things that were impossible to predict. Our merger was now only weeks away from a St.George

---

25   In the light of my previous role, and for reasons of good governance, I did not participate in decisions regarding price, nor in matters to do with due diligence.

shareholder vote and both courage and confidence were required to push ahead. 'We know what we are doing. Let's finish what we've started' was what we agreed.

On 1 December 2008, the transaction was concluded. The entities were now merged. Let the delivery begin: $400 million of cost synergies, $175 million of revenue benefits, $100 million of funding benefits over a three-year period. Our explicit goal was for the transaction to be earnings-per-share accretive by the third year. On the whole, the market was sceptical to negative on the transaction, either believing that in the midst of the financial crisis we should not have taken on such a big bite, or that we had paid too much and should have waited.

The scepticism only grew as we outlined and then implemented the business model for the merged entity. It explicitly allowed for the retention of the St.George and BankSA brands and all their branches. While head offices, operational areas and product functions would be merged, we planned to run what we called at the time a 'multi-brand model'[26] on the basis of providing choice to customers. We would not, as occurred in conventional in-market mergers, be forcing St.George and BankSA customers to adopt Westpac as their bank. While cost synergies are high when branches are closed and brands are withdrawn, customers don't like to be told what to do, and when they are, market-share loss occurs. I knew that St.George customers loved their bank. They would not forgive us if we destroyed it. A quick calculation showed that the value of these customers far outweighed the cost savings that could be made by closing branches and shutting down brands. Our plan

---

26 'Multi-brand' proved to be a poor choice of words. The strategy was not to run and manage several brands. Rather, it was to provide choice to customers, recognising the distinctive positioning of each brand. We adjusted for this in 2012 and dropped the term.

was to grow customer numbers and deepen relationships. 'Don't lose a single customer' was the early call to action for the organisation. This was Brad Cooper's phrase – Brad being the talented executive I selected for the role of chief transformation officer.

One of the first things we did after announcing the merger was write an open letter to customers. While explicitly directed to Westpac customers, it was, in reality, also written for the customers of St.George.

To all our customers

Gail Kelly CEO Westpac

It is now a month since we first announced the proposed merger between St.George and Westpac. What I would like to do is to share with you, via this open letter, our vision for the future and the ways in which this union will benefit customers of both St.George and Westpac.

It is important to note that we are approaching this in a very different way from prior mergers within Australia. Our vision, and my personal passion, is one of putting customers at the centre, working hard to deepen relationships and improve the service experience. We want to be a bank that earns all our customers' business.

This means that we will continue to respect your choices. We will retain, and enhance, both St.George and Westpac brands, and our customer touchpoints, even if the branches are right alongside each other. We will retain our branches and St.George's, including in regional and rural Australia. Most importantly, this means that the wonderful employees from both St.George and Westpac, whom you know and deal with day-to-day, won't change.

One key benefit that we will be able to offer from the outset is that both St.George and Westpac's customers will be able to use each other's ATMs (over 2,700 in total) without paying any additional fees.

Over time, we expect that, through an integrated and enhanced operating platform, we will be able to offer the best of both products and services.

A united St.George and Westpac will be Australia's largest financial services company and will be well placed to meet the challenges that the world's economies are now facing. We will have a strong credit rating and be well positioned to compete here with overseas and local banks, and to offer the security you deserve and need.

You will find more information on the merger at **westpac.com.au/merger** and please do not hesitate to contact me directly at **gailkellyCEO@westpac.com.au** to share your thoughts. I would love to hear from you.

Thank you for your support.

Gail Kelly

Westpac

© Westpac Banking Corporation (ABN 33 007 457 141).

The model we were pursuing was unconventional and bold, but it was right. This was how to make a merger with St.George work. St.George's biggest strengths lay in its friendly service culture and its loyal customer base. It was obvious to me that we should do everything we could to protect and reinforce its culture, while also using the strength of the Westpac Group to provide additional products and services. We were able to promote the fact that as a consequence of the merger, St.George had the benefit of an 'AA' rating behind it. From a Westpac Group point of view, the merger accelerated our customer-centred transformation. St.George provided technology such as its teller and call-centre systems that was urgently required in Westpac. It was also more customer-friendly in a number of its service processes, complaint management being a good example. Overall, the fact that we were absolutely clear on our agenda set us up for success. It helped us hold the course through the next few difficult years.

Between 2008 and 2012, the market continued to be sceptical. And so launching a new brand, Bank of Melbourne, and running it as part of the St.George group of brands certainly took courage. The business case stacked up. Melburnians did not have a serious alternative to the major banks, as Bendigo Bank was more regional in its focus.[27] We already owned the Bank of Melbourne brand name,[28] and our research showed that customers regarded it with deep affection. In contrast, to the extent that St.George was recognised within Victoria, it was seen as a New South Wales bank. Our strategy was to replace St.George in Victoria with Bank of Melbourne, rebranding existing branches and business-banking centres with

---

27   Detailed empirical research revealed that 30 per cent of Australians would prefer to bank with a local or regional bank, all other things being equal.

28   Bank of Melbourne, a regional bank established in 1957, had been acquired by Westpac in 1997. It was later integrated into Westpac and the brand name was dropped.

a new and contemporary look. Our relaunched Bank of Melbourne would be innovative and bold, with employees carefully selected for their customer-service orientation. It would have a dedicated call centre and an engaging social media profile. It would be technologically savvy. A strong local CEO would be selected, with real authority to make customer-centred decisions. We planned to have 100 branches in operation in five years, 70 more than the starting position. We believed a 10 per cent retail market share was achievable in the medium term, up from its current 2.5 per cent. This would be a bank for Victorians, a vibrant and competitive local alternative operating only within Victoria.

We knew at the outset that we would be criticised. We expected that certain analysts and media commentators would be negative about the cost implications of opening more branches and launching a new brand; that they would focus on the risks of existing Westpac customers leaving to join the new bank rather than the opportunity of winning customers from our competitors. Nevertheless, we backed ourselves to deliver. Decision day arrived and we presented the strategic rationale and business case to the board. A number of board members were lukewarm, but the tide turned when Lindsay Maxsted, himself a Victorian and later to become Westpac's chairman, memorably commented: 'Just pin your ears back and do it!'

On 10 March 2011 the new venture was launched. Our media release boldly proclaimed: 'Today we are delighted to announce the launch of a new bank in Victoria during August 2011 – Bank of Melbourne!'

Seven years on, it is clear that our courage and determination paid off. The numbers show that the St.George merger successfully transformed the Westpac Group. It did, however, take longer than we would have liked, and 2011–12 in particular were difficult years. The St.George brand was plateauing and at risk of losing its culture of innovation and customer service. Employees were disheartened and it seemed to me that they had lost their positive spirit of engagement and down-to-earth approach. They had become passive. At a 'town hall' meeting of St.George leaders, I shocked them with the force of my words: 'What has happened to you? Where is your passion? Where is your energy? Where is the St.George I know – the bank of warm, friendly, committed, can-do people who go the extra mile for customers? You need to fight. Don't just accept things.' The feedback stung and key individuals stepped up.

This was also the time that I appointed George Frazis as St.George's new CEO. George brought with him deep retail experience, a passion for customers and innovation, and a strong results orientation. Importantly, he brought a preparedness and confidence to take on the bigger brother, Westpac, which sometimes was required. St.George employees responded instantly to George's energy and personal leadership style. The numbers say it all: in the period from 2012 to 2015, cash earnings for St.George Banking Group grew from $1.2 billion to $1.7 billion. At the time of the merger, total customer numbers stood at around three million; by 2015, St.George had 3.8 million customers. In terms of consumer satisfaction and NPS, St.George was consistently ahead of all the major banks.

As for the Bank of Melbourne, it was off to a very good start. We had a first-class CEO in Scott Tanner, a Melburnian through and through. Under his leadership, the bank achieved its five-year goals in four years. Customer numbers grew from 220 000 at launch in

2011 to over 500 000 in 2016. Growth in customer deposits and in mortgage lending was particularly impressive – as much as two to three times the rate of growth of the rest of the market. What makes this sustainable is that Bank of Melbourne has become the 'main bank', the 'this is my bank', for a growing number of Victorians who prefer a vibrant, service-driven local alternative.

Managing a portfolio of brands all at different stages of development with differing priorities is not a simple thing, and over time we became more experienced and better equipped to manage the complexity. The one-size-fits-all approach does not work. The model requires strong leaders who are bold and creative, yet understand fundamentally that they are part of a team. For any single leader to succeed, the team as a whole needs to win.

Let me conclude this section by drawing the threads together. Courage is a leadership quality. In my case, as the stories of the St.George merger and the reintroduction of the Bank of Melbourne show, this particular quality does not stand on its own. It is inextricably linked to drive and determination. It involves clarity of vision and preparedness to tough it out. It is backed up by careful research and meticulous planning. Its effective deployment depends crucially on having the right people in the right roles, bringing their intellect, judgement, skills and energy to deliver team goals.

Taken together the program of work we undertook at Westpac in those years from 2008 to 2014 was both enormous in scale and enormous in risk. A financial crisis, a major merger, a transformation around customers, an overhaul of our technology – this was not for the faint-hearted. Of course, the magnitude of what we were undertaking was not apparent at first. The crucial thing is that we did not blink or doubt ourselves. I am immensely proud of the team. Board members, executives and employees across the Group – we remained focused on our vision and goals, and aligned in our implementation. Whatever was thrown at us, we just kept going.

5

DELIVER
RESULTS

A leader's effectiveness is measured by the results that are delivered, not only over the period the leader is in charge, but also once he or she has left. High-quality, sustainable delivery is the goal. Many elements pulling together, including luck, produce this outcome. While the chapters in this book cover a number of these elements, the ability to deliver results is so crucially important that I have given it its own focus.

Here are the lessons I have learned.

1. Short-termism is a damaging drug

This first point provides a caution: beware of the insidious pressures that mount to deliver short-term results whatever the cost. Such pressures include the market's seemingly shorter and shorter time horizon, the 24-hour news cycle with its relentless focus on current-day performance, and a push to achieve financial outcomes that deliver short-term bonuses. Falling captive to these pressures leads to decisions that 'short-term' the business:

- 'That investment in our payments architecture – I'm sure it can wait until next year.'
- 'We've invested a lot in training over the years; I think we can cut back on it now.'
- 'For this last quarter of the year, let's implement a hiring freeze and not replace frontline employees who leave.'
- 'We can't afford to spend so much on IT maintenance. We'll need to get by without it for a year or two.'
- 'Why don't we capitalise more of our investments so we don't incur the cost now?'
- 'I propose we extend the life of our assets.'
- 'Just tell the regulatory affairs team that they are going to have to do more with less. We're cutting their budget.'

Heard any of these? Watch out for them, and shout out loudly. They represent the slippery slope and are an anathema to a culture focused on customers.

2. Inculcate a 'Both . . . and' philosophy

One of my favourite discussion points with general management teams was what I called the 'Both . . . and' approach.

The opposite of this, the 'either-or' mindset, is often unnecessarily limiting. Things that on the surface appear to be at opposite ends can, in reality, sit comfortably alongside each other, and even reinforce each other. Favourites for me include 'productivity and quality' and 'sales and service'. Executives may fall into the trap of thinking that a productivity or cost-management focus will come at the expense of quality; or that a sales focus means that service to customers will be compromised. On the contrary, a well-executed productivity strategy will eliminate errors and rework, effectively re-designing processes. It will have the effect of enhancing quality. Similarly, a sales strategy needs to start with a full understanding of the customer's needs in order to ensure that whatever is offered is in the customer's best interests. As I often discussed with St.George frontline staff, sales and service go hand in hand.

Delivering both in the short term and the long term is another one of these 'Both . . . ands', and can be achieved without the short-termism I so strongly caution against. Executives preparing three- and five-year forecasts often presented me with a 'hockey stick' plan – an immediate period of significantly lower results followed by a steep ramp-up in later years. I never found these plans believable. Back to the drawing board we would go, examining the mix of investments and their payback periods, reviewing past investments to ensure that planned benefits were indeed materialising, and freshly reviewing revenue opportunities and areas for productivity enhancement. I would remind the team of the Alice quote in Lewis Carroll's *Through the Looking-Glass, and What Alice Found There*: Speaking to Alice, the Queen stated:

'The rule is, jam tomorrow and jam yesterday – but never jam *today.*'

'It *must* come sometimes to "jam today",' Alice objected.

'No, it can't,' said the Queen. 'It's jam every *other* day: today isn't any *other* day, you know.'

I'm with Alice. Jam today *and* jam tomorrow – that's what we need. For the most part, it is what we achieved.

3. Drive a high-performance culture

I am cautious about using the term 'high-performance culture' as it has become somewhat of a management buzz-phrase. I have seen hard-nosed business executives talk with passion and pride of how they have ruthlessly applied its techniques. Set high goals, ensure clear accountability, track, measure, reward and sanction – all well and good except it can lead to an environment of fear, intimidation and intolerance for difference. The culture becomes one where only the outcomes matter, not the processes of how they were achieved. Under pressure to perform, distortion or, even worse, manipulation of outcomes may be the result.

What happened at Wells Fargo is a case in point. This is a bank that was widely recognised for consistent superior performance. Amongst the major US banks, it was the one least affected by the financial crisis of 2008–09. Indeed, it was a bank that I admired and respected. Yet something went wrong. In what turned out to be a pressure-cooker of a sales culture, over 5000 employees across the company opened accounts for fictitious customers or sold products that actual customers did not want or need. They knew they were doing the wrong thing, and yet under pressure from their managers they did it. The narrow focus of the extremely stretch-ing cross-sell goals and the incentivisation that went with it, had become what mattered. Senior executives were slow to pick up the signals to understand that they were dealing with a serious systemic issue and to take personal responsibility for what had happened. The high-performance formula that had been so successful for so long had itself become the issue.

What can we learn from this? For leaders of the future, what should a culture of high performance involve? From my per-spective, the foundational elements are clarity of purpose, right people in the right roles and generous-spirited leadership. High-performance leaders set clear and challenging expectations and hold themselves to account. They are explicit in their articulation of not just what needs to get done, but also of why it matters. They ensure that everyone understands that doing the right thing is what is expected, that acting in the customer's best interests is the imper-ative. These leaders then allow individuals to play to their strengths. They look to create an environment where employees can flourish, where they feel supported and encouraged. Learning is fostered. When employees understand the purpose of the firm, are clear in how they can contribute, and are backed to give of their best, they bring discretionary effort to the task. The result: ordinary people achieving extraordinary results.

4. The power of a bold goal

Setting a bold goal and achieving alignment behind it can be trans-formative for performance. By November 2012, I knew that I needed a circuit-breaker. Our performance as a Group over the pre-vious 18 months had been disappointing. It was taking a lot longer than I would have liked for the benefits of our St.George merger and our customer-centred strategy to be evident in our results. I was failing in my communication to the market. Feedback from analysts and investors expressed concern over the sluggish trajectory of our earnings-per-share growth and the declining trend of our return on equity (ROE). My chairman, Lindsay Maxsted, and deputy chairman, John Curtis, gave me both feedback and advice. My team gave me their support.

At our 2012 full-year results presentation on 5 November, I surprised the market by publicly announcing a new goal – I indicated that I was putting a 'line in the sand' on ROE, and that the line in the sand was 15 per cent. Anything less than this could be marked up as a fail. At that point, our ROE was standing at 15.5 per cent, and had been 16 per cent the year before. My 15 per cent 'line in the sand' goal was a bold one that my own team had counselled me against.[29] What if we missed? What if things were worse than we thought? But I had decided it was time to put reputations on the line, including my own. It was an 'on the bus' moment made possible because I knew I had a committed team who would support me. Indeed, the 15 per cent 'line in the sand' goal became a rallying cry internally, a substantial call to action. Making key portfolio decisions and determining where capital should be deployed became easier. General managers took accountability for the returns in their business. The power of productivity, of doing more with what we had, was embraced. Across the company, our employees enthusiastically stepped up to drive our customer-service strategy, focusing on winning more customers and deepening relationships.

---

29   The goal was a bold one because across the banking industry, ROEs were on a declining trend for a number of reasons. Regulatory requirements to hold much higher levels of capital was the single biggest factor.

A year later, at our 2013 full-year results presentation, I was able to announce an ROE of 16 per cent. In November 2014, it was 16.4 per cent. This bold goal had proved to be very powerful indeed.

5. Resource allocation

I have learned many lessons over the years with regard to resource allocation decisions. The list of potential opportunities is always much longer than the list of initiatives that can be successfully delivered to conclusion. Where and how the leader chooses to invest is crucial to long-term success. My experience has been hard-won. A few things I have learned are:

- When signing off on a set of initiatives, it is important to explicitly say no to others and make sure that any resources already in place are reallocated. In my experience, projects that are not explicitly killed off either go into hiding or have a tendency to limp along, absorbing valuable management time.
- It is better to focus on a few big things than on lots of small things. Resource allocation is about trade-offs and choices. Maximum focus needs to be placed on the initiatives that matter most to the strategic agenda and provide the best long-term return on capital. Being even-handed among executives or divisions is not the goal.
- A disciplined and rigorous approach is required when evaluating different opportunities. Trade-offs need to be explicit. For example, at Westpac we thought about our business in terms of four main areas of focus: growth, strength, return and productivity. We had measurable goals for each area but knew that there were trade-offs inherent in

our decisions. An initiative that would enhance our strength, such as lengthening our funding profile, would reduce our ROE, so would come at a cost. A program focused on growth, for example, opening new branches in Shanghai and in Mumbai, would reduce our overall returns in the short and medium term but would be strategically important to support our Australian customers who do business in China and India. A focus on productivity could well support bottom-line results but come at the cost of growth, as investment dollars were prioritised away from marketing and sales.

- Carefully assess issues of do-ability and interdependencies. Inexperienced or overly optimistic executives tend to underestimate the change management and costs involved in the implementation of significant programs. Indeed sometimes, in order to make a business case work, they blindly work backwards from the required answer. The cumulative effect of change is also frequently ignored or understated. In Westpac's retail bank, we had to carefully think through the 'landing impacts' of virtually simultaneous implementations of a new business model for our branches, new appointments to bank manager roles, redesigned measurement systems, the implementation of a new teller system and a new customer relationship management (CRM) approach. Cumulatively, this was a truckload of change for frontline staff to deal with. It would be easy to underestimate the extent of training required, as well as the likely negative impact on sales and service over the transitional period. We multiplied the change management effort by ten, more than doubled the financial contingency, and re-phased the implementation agenda. That was the minimum required for success.

- Put your very best people on the most important projects. These people typically need to be full-time deployed. Rob Whitfield in leading the St.George merger planning and negotiations, Peter Hanlon and Jason Yetton in running the Twenty17 program to redesign our Westpac sales and service delivery, Scott Tanner in leading the Bank of Melbourne program, Bob McKinnon for our very ambitious technology agenda – these are great examples of right people, right skills for critically important programs. When I reflect on where we ran into difficulty, I recognise that it was often this essential ingredient that was missing.

- Productivity programs deliver more successfully if they incorporate a growth component. Not surprisingly, executives and employees engage more energetically for a 'Save to invest' type of program than a 'Manage costs' one.

6. One Team

A 'One Team' approach is different from teamwork. It is richer and stronger in its meaning. One Team involves everyone in the organisation thinking and acting as One Team – across silos, across hierarchies, people all pulling together to serve customers. I love this definition. It implies that team members will do whatever it takes without looking for individual credit. They will never stand back and say, 'That's not my role' or 'That's not my fault'. On the back of this learning, we changed our Westpac value of 'Teamwork' to 'One Team' and laid out a set of behaviours to bring the concept to life. We rewarded and celebrated the individuals demonstrating these behaviours in action. As an executive team, we tested ourselves. Once a decision is made, are we 100 per cent aligned behind it? Does each one of us communicate it with passion and vigour, even if in the cut and thrust of the decision-making process we argued for a different answer? Does each one of us actively support our colleagues, going to their assistance when things are difficult, being prepared to reallocate resources, even at our own cost? Do we have each other's backs? As we practised, we got better at it, and as we got better, the results got better too.

In talking about this internally, I sometimes used the analogy of top-quality sporting teams who embody a One Team philosophy. In the game of cricket, for example, team members have very specific roles: opening batsman, first-wicket-down or No.3 batsman, all-rounder, wicket-keeper, fast bowler, different types of spin bowlers, and so on. Yet each will do whatever is required in the context of the game to win. A batsman may be required to score very quickly from the first ball and so put his wicket at risk; the order of batsmen coming in may need to be changed depending on the state of the game; in a run-out mix-up, a batsman may need to sacrifice his wicket in order to keep his in-form partner at the crease. Each player is intuitively thinking and acting 'One Team' – not his individual performance or his individual statistics. He will willingly do what it takes for the team as a whole to deliver. Just as in sport, getting this right in business is extremely powerful. It drives alignment, engagement and superior outcomes.

7. Decision-making

Lack of decision-making paralyses the team. Slow, clunky processes surrounding decision-making frustrate the team. Decisions that are syndicated, where too many people take on the right of veto, drive a culture of 'All care and no responsibility'. To achieve results, to drive outcomes, the leader needs to make clear, timely decisions and stand behind them.

Making decisions has never been a problem for me. The important thing I had to work out was what decisions were mine to make, and which were best made by others. Early in my leadership career, I fell into the trap of taking on the decisions my team could or should be making, either because I failed to properly delegate and empower or, just as bad, because I allowed 'upward delegation' to occur. I became wiser as my leadership matured, and fortunately this coincided with my judgement and instinct for things maturing too.

In the role of CEO, particularly on issues of strategic importance, my decision-making style involved broad consultation. I would encourage team debate and a robust exchange of views. I would seek to understand the facts of the situation as fully as possible and engage in more informal 'tossing around' of the issues with trusted advisers both inside and outside the bank.

'What if . . .?'

'Can this be right?'

'Am I thinking about this properly?'

'What am I missing?'

'Can you clearly explain why you think that?'

'How might this play out if our key assumption proves to be wrong?'

'What other options do we have?'

'How will the market respond?'

'What would you do?'

'How should I communicate this?'

These and many more were the type of questions I would bounce around with individuals, very happy to be the 'student' when the adviser had greater experience and knowledge. Through this process of iteration and debate, and after quiet personal reflection, I would come to a decision. I would try to be very clear with myself why I had landed at that point. I would then communicate the call. Depending on the nature of the decision and the circumstances, I could circle back to team members individually or as a group. Either way, I was confident that I would be backed.

There are, of course, many ways of setting about making key decisions. Leadership styles differ, circumstances differ. On some occasions, it is really helpful to achieve a consensus decision. On others, leading from the front with courage is required. My major point is that making clear, timely decisions matters to the delivery of results. It really matters. Teams want certainty and clarity of direction, and they look to the leader to provide it. Only once the decision is made can execution begin.

8. Relentless focus

Leaders who are passionate about delivering results are never complacent. They bring a relentless focus to what they do. Day in, day out, they pay attention to the detail, celebrate the small wins and pivot quickly to where problems exist. The leader's attention and focus drive the organisation's attention and focus. A disciplined operating rhythm of managing performance is the result. Delivery becomes a habit. Planning, preparing, executing, following up, learning, reinforcing, always looking to improve, unwavering commitment to high performance – this is the relentless focus that leaders who consistently deliver bring to what they do. A piece of research conducted by McKinsey & Co. and published in January 2015 as 'Decoding Leadership: What Really Matters' concluded that a small subset of leadership skills most closely correlated with leadership success. McKinsey's comprehensive research into 81 different types of organisations revealed that four kinds of behaviour accounted for 89 per cent of leadership effectiveness. I was not surprised to read that one of those four was 'Operate with a strong results orientation'.[30]

---

30 The other three were: 'Be supportive', 'Seek different perspectives' and 'Solve problems effectively'.

6

GENEROSITY
OF SPIRIT

If I had written a book on life and leadership lessons ten years ago, I would have called this chapter 'Working through and with people'. Under this heading, I would have addressed the topics of motivating others, delegation, and working effectively in teams. I would even have drawn from my MBA research report of 1986 entitled 'Chief Executive Officer Success and the Development of High Potential Employees'. This work involved extensive desktop research into leadership thinking that was current at the time, as well as empirical research into the practices of South Africa's leading CEOs, each of whom was widely acknowledged to have achieved success. Among the 25 I interviewed were Raymond Ackerman (Pick 'n Pay), Chris Ball (Barclays National Bank), Warren Clewlow (Barlow Rand), Meyer Kahn (South African Breweries), Sol Kerzner (Sun International), Bob Tucker (South African Permanent Building Society) and Conrad Strauss (Standard Bank of South Africa).

The key conclusion of the study was how important it is to work with and through people. This factor emerged as more crucial than personal drive, dealing with change, courage, having a clear vision, and industry experience. Each of the CEOs spoke with energy on the topic, exploring themes of how to motivate, empower, delegate and communicate. Comments such as the following are typical of those made:

'I had to learn to manage through a wide variety of people. If I could not do this, I would not be able to deliver.'
'At the end of the road, you are only as good as the people that work for you and with you.'

As important as all these points are, I recognise that they are not enough. For me, the financial crisis raised the question of what makes a great leader. As discussed in Chapter 2 of this part of the book, having a strong understanding of the organisation's purpose is critical, together with the ability to communicate and to build alignment. In addition, how the leader behaves in his or her engagement with others is something I started to reflect upon. The conclusion I reached is that being an outstanding leader of people starts with having a deep respect for each individual and a belief in the power of each person to make a difference. This respect and belief provide the foundation for how to lead. Instead of talking of 'working with and through people', I now talk of 'generosity of spirit'.

In simple terms, the generous-spirited leader has a genuine desire for the individual to flourish and a strong drive to assist team members to be the best they can be. He or she creates an environment where people can perform fearlessly, where they can grow and develop. This style of leadership is not selfish or quick to judge. It involves deep listening and seeks to walk in the shoes of others. Generous-spirited leaders are visible and authentic. Because they care, they are kind and compassionate. They are also self-aware. If you are self-aware, you are able to directly engage in an activity while at the same time stand back and observe yourself. 'Dancing on the dancefloor while simultaneously observing myself from the upper balcony' is sometimes how I describe it. I understand my impact on others; I am fully in the moment.

It frequently surprises me how oblivious senior executives are to the fact that their everyday behaviour is closely watched, that they cast long shadows. Senior leadership behaviour directly influences culture. The financial crisis of recent years, devastating in its impact on the lives of so many people, exposed the deficiencies of banking CEOs. Many were found to be out of touch, aloof and arrogant. Employees lived in fear of their bosses. Not surprisingly, banking cultures reflected this behaviour.

When I consider leaders I have encountered in my life journey, the individual who best embodied 'generosity of spirit' was Nelson Mandela. I recall being riveted in front of the television screen in our Parkview home in Johannesburg on the morning of 11 February 1990 when Mandela walked out of prison, proud and tall, with his wife Winnie at his side. Later that day, Allan and I listened to his address delivered from the balcony of the City Hall in Cape Town. This was the first time we had seen live pictures of Nelson Mandela, or heard his voice.

In 1964, as an outcome of the Rivonia Trial in Johannesburg, Mandela and several other leaders of the African National Congress (ANC) were sentenced to life imprisonment on Robben Island. So began his 27 years of incarceration, including spells in solitary confinement. Over this period, the South African Nationalist government became ever harsher and more zealous in their management of the apartheid system. The 1980s were the very worst of years. After the Soweto riots of 1976 and the assassination of Steve Biko in 1977, the struggle for liberation intensified. Censorship, bannings, detention without trial, surveillance and phone tapping were among the tools of the ruling party. And while we later learned that the negotiations for Mandela's release had been underway for some period, the apparent speediness of the actual release came as a surprise.

What sort of leader would Mandela be? What did the future hold? Certainly, in light of the extended period of acute oppression, injustice and systematic discrimination, it would not have been unreasonable to expect bitterness and a drive for revenge. But Mandela's very first speech provided early insight into the heart of this extraordinary leader. He spoke of peace and democracy and freedom for all. He said he stood before us a humble servant of the people, and that he placed the remaining years of his life in our hands. His was a voice of hope.

On Tuesday 10 May 1994, Mandela was inaugurated president of South Africa. He was solemn, full of dignity and calmness, deeply aware of his journey so far, fully cognisant that his task of rebuilding a nation had just begun. In his autobiography, he writes beautifully of this realisation:

> I have walked that long road to freedom. I have tried not to falter; I have made missteps along the way. But I have discovered the secret that after climbing a great hill, one only finds that there are many more hills to climb. I have taken a moment here to rest, to steal a view of the glorious vista that surrounds me, to look back on the distance I have come. But I can rest only for a moment, for with freedom come responsibilities, and I dare not linger, for my long walk is not yet ended.

The years immediately following the birth of 'the New South Africa' were truly remarkable. South Africans of all races and creeds experienced transformative leadership in action. President Mandela had a clear vision for his nation – a vision that united all South Africans in a peaceful democracy. He explained: 'I knew that people expected me to harbor resentment towards whites. But I had none. In prison, my anger towards whites decreased, but my hatred for the system grew. I wanted South Africa to see that I loved even my enemies while I hated the system that turned us against one another.' In Mandela's New South Africa, there was a place for everyone who embraced the values of freedom for all. As president, he not only communicated this at every turn, but also used symbols and actions to show he was serious.

A sporting highlight of my life was attending the final of the 1995 Rugby World Cup at Ellis Park in Johannesburg – a gripping, extremely tense game between traditional rivals the Springboks and the All Blacks, where in extra time, thanks to a Joel Stransky drop goal, the Springboks prevailed. Out onto the turf strode Nelson Mandela, president of South Africa, wearing a Springbok jersey with the number 6 on its back – the jersey of the team's captain, Francois Pienaar. As Pienaar raised the trophy aloft, Mandela was cheering at his side. The stadium erupted – 63 000 people, 62 000 of them white, many Afrikaans, chanting 'Nelson! Nelson! Nelson!' It was electric. And standing there, being swept on the wave of euphoria, I had to pinch myself to think that this was rugby, the passion of the oppressive National Party. This was the sport rejected by most black South Africans. It was the very symbol of apartheid. Travelling home from the match I saw South Africans black and white celebrating alongside each other, waving flags, hooting, singing and dancing in the streets in a new unity inspired by generosity of spirit, one to the other. It was extraordinary.

Mandela was renowned for his personal warmth, his care and respect for individuals, his taking time to acknowledge and thank, his ability to be in the moment. He sought to walk in the shoes of others in order to understand their perspectives and points of view. He listened, properly listened, and was not quick to judge. He embraced reconciliation. Many examples can be found. He reached out to Dr Percy Yutar, the chief prosecutor in the Rivonia Trial of 1963–64. He invited one of his former jailers to his inauguration in 1994, and travelled to meet and have tea with Betsie Verwoerd, whose husband, Hendrik Verwoerd, had been the architect of the apartheid system in 1948. Against the spirited advice of many, he made the decision to retain the Springbok emblem for the sport of rugby. At the national level, he established the Truth and Reconciliation Commission under the chairmanship of Bishop Desmond Tutu. The emphasis of this commission was to bring out the truth of apartheid's dark years and dark acts, and seek to provide some level of cleansing and closure for both victims and perpetrators. Bishop Tutu wrote of how moved he was by the extraordinary generosity of spirit shown by victims towards their tormentors: '. . . retribution wounds and divides us from one another. Only restoration can heal us and make us whole. And only forgiveness enables us to restore trust and compassion to our relationships. If peace is our goal, there can be no future without forgiveness.'

Coming out of apartheid, South Africa and South Africans were very lucky to have Nelson Mandela – *Madiba*[31] – as their new president. The most authentic and generous-spirited of men, he was a powerful leader.

Mandela's story is one I frequently told as I discussed insights of leadership and worked to introduce generous-spirited leadership into the bank. As a Westpac executive team, we appreciated that generosity of spirit needed to start with us, with our behaviour towards each other. In 2009, we held the first of what became a regular event – an offsite team meeting focused exclusively on culture and behaviours. We spent time on our own, in pairs, and with the team as a whole. We shared elements of our individual journeys, including personal visions for ourselves and for our organisation. We developed a charter that would govern our behaviours.

31   *Madiba* is a term of endearment that many South Africans use for Mandela. According to the Nelson Mandela Foundation, Madiba was the name of a chief who ruled in the Transkei in the 18th century.

This agreement became a background document attached to the papers for executive team meetings and included sections on 'Our Purpose', 'What We Will Be Known For' and 'Our Behaviours'.

The 'Our Behaviours' section read as follows:

We commit individually and as a team to role-model our values and demonstrate:

Generosity of spirit through:
>> Assuming good intent
>> Encouraging and helping others to flourish
>> Being tolerant of differences
>> Looking for opportunities to help each other

Strong relationships through:
>> Getting to know each other well
>> Making time for each other and being responsive to requests
>> Dealing with difficult issues or potential conflict face to face
>> Being advocates for each other and having each other's backs
>> Having fun

High-quality, rigorous debate through:
>> Being present 'in the moment'
>> Providing insights and helping each other focus on the things that make a difference
>> Obligation to constructive dissent
>> Being courageous and making tough calls
>> Cabinet solidarity once decisions are made

In our team offsites, typically held half-yearly, we allocated time to check in on how we were doing. Ahead of each offsite, we would rate ourselves on our performance and obtain feedback from a selection of our general managers. This was collated and presented back to us. Then, sitting in a circle, each of us shared personal reflections on areas we were working on, and received comments and suggestions from colleagues. This took courage and was often quite confronting.

As a team, we were ambitious for our company, we competed strongly in the marketplace and we wanted to win. We understood that to do so required setting high standards, holding ourselves to account and empowering our people. It required getting into the trenches when necessary – supporting, encouraging, communicating, coaching. It required alignment and cohesion at every level, but most importantly alignment between ourselves. We never stopped trying to get this right.

We also set out to apply 'generosity of spirit' behaviours to the way we handled performance reviews. Currently, the efficacy of performance reviews is being evaluated, with some companies deciding to do away with them. I believe they have a role, but it is a question of how they are done. The critical factor is not depending upon official reviews to give feedback and provide coaching. If you, as leader, are unhappy or concerned about some element of a team member's performance or behaviour, don't wait: deal with it in person and immediately. Similarly, if something has gone really well, acknowledge it. This is the right and fair thing to do. People should never receive surprises at the half-yearly or end-of-year review. Such reviews should be encouraging and useful rather than encounters to be endured. If at all possible, they should be face to face, either in person or via video conference. In my experience, discussions can usefully centre on:

> What are you most proud of over the past period?
> What were the lowlights of the period?
> What would you do differently?
> What have you learned?
> For the period ahead, what are your four or five key priorities?
> What are the biggest challenges you face?
> Do you have a robust plan?
> How can I help?
> Is there any specific development or support that you may need?

The session should always include the leader reinforcing the key strengths the individual brings to the role, acknowledging their contribution, teasing out the lessons to be learned and behaviours to be worked on, and providing encouragement in the tackling of personal hurdles. My approach was to produce a single-page document summarising the conversation, and attaching this to the self-assessment that each team member produced ahead of time. If the individual could walk out of my office with his or her shoulders back, feeling motivated, acknowledged, listened to, with a plan of attack for the next period, I felt this was a job well done.

It is important to note that there is nothing soft about generous-spirited leadership. Over my career, I have frequently met leaders who would describe themselves as Tough But Fair. There doesn't need to be a 'But'. A generous-spirited leader is Tough And Fair; he or she is Tough And Kind. Strong feedback will be given when required; a decision to mark down a remuneration outcome, to demote, or to ask an executive to leave will be made if deemed right, and will be handled sensitively, in person, and with due consideration for the team member's position. A mature, generous-spirited leader will take on the tough stuff and do it well. Operating from a position of deep respect for people, this style of leader will reflect not only on what is right for the business, but also on its impact on people. Tough And Fair, Tough And Kind – that is what the leader will be.

I am passionate about this leadership approach. It works because it is built on consistency, authenticity and trust. It is not about being liked or being nice. It is about a deeply held value system that is based on the position that people matter – they matter a lot. Every person, the most senior or the most junior, male or female, young or old, holding similar views to your own or different views, performing in their role or struggling – each one deserves your full respect. This is much more than a business leadership model: it is a model for living your life. Without doubt, it can be practised and learned. Kindness, compassion, consideration for others, tolerance, thoughtfulness, being in the moment – it seems to me that we need a lot more of this in the political sphere, across communities and in our day-to-day lives. It starts with a deep respect for others, and holding ourselves to a higher standard of behaviour.

7

DIVERSITY IS STRENGTH

In my view, corporate Australia tends to define 'diversity' too narrowly. A focus on diversity is translated into a focus on gender equality. Progress in this area has been disappointingly slow, and much more is required. Diversity, however, has a wider remit. Cultural and racial backgrounds, socioeconomic status, experience paths, age differences, sexual orientation, physical differences, religious views and ways of thinking – all these and more contribute to diversity. Building an inclusive organisation and fully harnessing these differences is extremely difficult, yet very powerful. Having a workforce more reflective of the society in which we live and the customers we serve enhances long-term sustainability, builds stronger alignment and facilitates better decision-making.

One might think that growing up in South Africa, I would have been exposed to diversity all my life. And yet that was not the case. Apartheid in South Africa drove strict separation rather than togetherness. Even the whites were divided into English- and Afrikaans-speaking groups by decades of mutual suspicion and bitterness. I grew up in a white suburb, went to a whites-only English-speaking girls' school and lived in an English-speaking neighbourhood. Outside of our wonderful housekeeper, Elizabeth Maseko, who lived on our property and supported the family over all the years we were in Pretoria, I did not know or engage with any black people. Such was the system we lived in. I am ashamed to have been part of it and, indeed, not to have challenged it more actively.

My experience with diversity deepened considerably in the mid to late 1980s and the 1990s. My MBA class of 1985–86 included a black student from Soweto. I learned firsthand from him of his life-long struggles. I was in awe of how he never failed to hand in his assignments and come prepared to lectures, notwithstanding his lengthy 'non-white only' bus and train commute. His small two-roomed home, which he shared with six to eight others, had no electricity and no toilet. His work was done by paraffin light.

I was also exposed to a number of activist lecturers, and my political consciousness expanded. These were truly dark and oppressive times in South Africa, with P.W. Botha as the National

Party leader.[32] In June 1986, in response to widespread unrest, a state of emergency was declared, giving the government even further powers. One afternoon that year, a group of us locked ourselves in a lecture theatre at the University of the Witwatersrand Business School to view a film on the history of the ANC. Everything to do with the ANC and its leaders was banned, and such a viewing was completely illegal. What I received was an education in South African history and in what it felt like to be afraid.

In the same year, 1986, Allan and I were returning from an international mortgage conference held in Cambridge, England, when we were stopped by the South African customs authorities at Johannesburg International Airport. Before flying home, we had visited Covent Garden and purchased two books: one a biography of Nelson Mandela, and the other a book on his wife, Winnie. The eyes of the customs officials lit up as they discovered this illicit material. They trashed our bags, emptying everything on the floor. The questioning then began. It was intimidating and belittling, and I suspect we got ourselves on a list somewhere of people to be observed. Allan's answer to the question of 'Why do you have these books?' only increased the hostility we faced. 'These are leaders in our country,' he said. 'It is important to get to know them and to understand our history.'

In late 1990, one year after the birth of our triplets, I took on the role of General Manager, Human Resources for the Perm, a division of the Nedcor Group. With Mandela newly released and a New South Africa in development, this was an exhilarating time to be in business. Under the progressive leadership of Bob Tucker,

---

32   P.W. Botha was known as 'Die Groot Krokodil' which literally translates as 'The Great Crocodile'. He was famous for his 1985 Rubicon speech, his threatening demeanour, his words 'Don't push us too far' and his wagging finger.

the Perm had long been in the vanguard of pushing for societal change. Now was the opportunity to drive this change in the organisation itself. My job involved the development and implementation of people strategies for the new world:

- Recruitment – including a strategy for bringing on board a number of returning political exiles.
- Training and development – due to the apartheid legacy, black South Africans had been starved of quality education. In addition, they had not been exposed to corporate environments. New skill sets were required.
- Organisational development and culture change – a massive task lay ahead in managing diversity, building an inclusive culture, and aligning people with very different backgrounds, experiences and fears around a common vision.
- Future workforce planning – paving the way for affirmative action targets.
- Industrial relations strategy – negotiating with unions and ensuring fairness and equality of opportunity.
- Community engagement – we adopted a strategy of local engagement where each branch and business banking centre took on a community project, for example, drilling boreholes, constructing roofs for classrooms, or providing after-hours teaching. We wanted to encourage people to get involved at a grassroots local level.

This personal development and exposure to diversity continued into my next role – head of the Nedcor Group card business. I was appointed to this position in 1992 and it was my first experience of running a profit-and-loss business. I was directly accountable for its 1000 employees, and therefore accountable for driving change and managing diversity in all its forms. A particular event stands out in my memory.

As background, the 1992–93 period was one of extreme violence, fear and strife across South Africa. Frequent ANC–Inkatha[33] clashes occurred, coupled with terror tactics by the white far-right wing, the AWB.[34] Chris Hani, the charismatic leader of the armed wing of the ANC (known as uMkhonto weSizwe), was assassinated, and Mandela appealed for calm. Around the same time, the Bisho massacre in the Ciskei, a nominal homeland state in the Eastern Cape, sent shockwaves around the country.[35] Twenty-eight ANC supporters died, and the South African government was widely believed to be responsible.

My offices, occupying eight floors in Biccard Street in Johannesburg, adjoined the Ciskei homeland offices. The day after the massacre, a highly charged demonstration took place in the street. Men and women in traditional dress, with traditional weapons, were *toyi-toying*[36] and singing, loudspeakers were blaring messages of incitement, people were marching, and buckets of animal blood were emptied on the street.

I joined a group of employees watching from our windows, then stood back for a moment and looked at the faces of the people around me. My team members were diverse in many ways: race group, political affiliation, educational background, life experience,

---

33 The Inkatha Freedom Party derived its support from the Zulu people of what is now KwaZulu-Natal. In the late 1980s and early 1990s, supporters of the two political forces, the ANC and Inkatha, were regularly involved in violent confrontations.

34 AWB stands for Afrikaner Weerstandsbeweging, or Afrikaner Resistance Movement.

35 As part of apartheid's policy of separate development, the National Party government had declared a number of black homelands to be independent states. The Ciskei was one of these, the others being the Transkei, Bophuthatswana and Venda.

36 *Toyi-toyi* is a South African word that describes a particular type of war dance. It became a key feature of anti-government protests.

age, gender. I saw the full range of emotions, including fear, anger, bitterness, panic and pride. At one point, a young black member of our team standing in front of me raised his arm in the Black Power salute and shouted excitedly, joining in with the chant below: 'One settler, one bullet'. The next minute he stepped back and inadvertently bumped into me, his white boss. He was immediately and genuinely full of apology and concern.

As I stood there, I reflected on the challenge ahead: how do we build a purpose and vision for our business and its people that will create meaning for us all, that will engage us and align us? I knew that getting it right was fundamental to our success. Diversity, if effectively harnessed and built on a platform of respect, tolerance and inclusion, is powerful. Unmanaged, it can be damaging and destructive.

In January 1996, my role at Nedcor Bank was broadened to include all retail and wealth-management products. In addition, I was given overall responsibility for Peoples Bank, a new bank we were launching to meet the needs of the sizeable, largely unbanked population who were now full citizens of the New South Africa. Peoples Bank emerged from the split of the Perm into two entities: Permanent Bank, serving the traditional customer base, and Peoples Bank, with a starting point of around 300 branches. Our model was one of absolute simplicity:

- no-frills transaction and savings products
- small, short-term loans (micro-loans) backed by employers[37]
- everything card-based
- no cheque accounts, credit cards or car financing
- fully leveraging the infrastructure, product set and technology of the rest of the group.

---

37   Employers were key – we provided payroll services to them and required them to underwrite the micro-loans for their employees.

This was a bold new venture that I was excited to be leading. I had a lot to learn, not only about trying to deliver a return from simple, low-cost banking to a sizeable small-balance customer base, but also about diversity. Together with Mike Leeming, the executive director of the bank, to whom I reported, we set about forming a team to run Peoples Bank. We aimed to achieve a mix of skills and appointed talented high-potential male and female black executives. In staffing the branches, we needed to better match employees with local customers. In different parts of the country that meant different things, with a strong Zulu population in Natal, Indian population in Durban, Xhosa population in the Eastern Cape and coloured[38] population in the Western Cape. We opened new branches to service traditional township areas, for example, in Soweto and Tembisa. In visiting those branches, with my white skin, blond hair and high-heeled shoes, I was aware of standing out from everyone around.

This was certainly banking with a difference. On paydays, queues for branches and their ATMs snaked for hundreds of metres around several street corners. Many customers were illiterate, which brought challenges for identification and providing service. Customers also brought deeply held cultural traditions to their banking. I recall visiting a Peoples Bank branch in Pinetown, Natal, where a customer sat on the floor, his sangoma or witchdoctor in front of him, as the bones were thrown. I was informed that the customer was seeking financial advice!

---

38 'Coloured' is the term used to describe people of mixed race. This population group is primarily located in the Western Cape.

In October 1997, I left for Australia to join the Commonwealth Bank, with Allan and the children following six weeks later. While Australia is rich in its diversity, this was not the case with respect to the Australian banking industry, a traditionally male domain. Westpac, Australia's oldest bank, appointed the first women in the industry. The 'lady typewriters', as they were called, were placed on 12 months' probation at an annual salary of £80 and worked in an area separated from the male staff. A few years ago, I read a fascinating letter from the bank's archives detailing the perceived perils of having women in banking. Written in June 1936 to the Bank Officers' Association (BOA), it stated:

> Females have no place in our association, which is an organisation for promoting professionalism amongst bank officers. The work of females is of inferior standard and they do not desire a banking career, but join the bank to make some pin money and to snare a husband. Doing so, they deny men of work. Their giggling and tittering disturbs the serious business of the banking chamber, makes customers uneasy and the junior clerks are distracted from their work. I urge you to reject their membership of the BOA, for to accept them would be to approve of their employment in the bank.

It was only in October 1961 that Westpac, then the Bank of New South Wales, employed its first full-time female teller,[39] mainly as a trial to 'gauge reaction of the public'. At that point the marriage bar, which restricted the employment of married women, was still

---

39   Twenty-five-year-old Judy Scott (nee Millar) was Westpac's first full-time teller, taking up her position at Sydney's Wynyard branch. Her appointment, on a trial basis only, generated a lot of publicity, not all of it positive.

in place. Female banking customers also suffered discrimination: male guarantors were an essential requirement before a bank would be prepared to provide a loan to a woman.

By 1997, despite societal changes and the implementation of hard-fought new legislation such as the Sex Discrimination Act of 1984 and the Affirmative Action Act of 1986, the Commonwealth Bank that I joined remained largely male-dominated, particularly in its senior ranks. It also lacked diversity in respect of experience and skill mix. David Murray was tackling this head on, and no doubt my own appointment reflected his push for greater levels of diversity. Change of this sort takes time, however, particularly in areas such as business banking. In late 1999 David appointed me to his executive team, giving me responsibility for the bank's retail and business-banking networks. Early on in that role, I called a conference of senior business-banking and credit executives from around the country. Around 150 people were there, and with the exception of myself, all were male, all were white, and almost all were long-standing CBA employees. Being a female and coming from South Africa, I felt like an outsider.

Across Australia, Westpac has been the pioneer in driving diversity. Helen Lynch was Australia's first female branch manager, appointed to the Rockhampton branch in 1978. She was also Australia's first female general manager in banking, appointed in 1989. Helen continued to play a groundbreaking role for women in Australia when she was appointed to Westpac's board in 1997.[40] Bob Joss, CEO of Westpac from 1993 to 1999, once famously said, 'Where are all the women?' as he set about aggressively pursuing change. Under David Morgan's strong advocacy the change agenda

---

40 The first woman to serve on the board of Westpac was the remarkable Eve Mahlab. She served from 1993 to 2001.

continued, with Ann Sherry,[41] Ilana Atlas and Sally Herman being among the female champions in the Group. A business called Women's Markets was established under the leadership of the irrepressible Larke Riemer to cater for the needs of female Australians, with a particular focus on women in small business. And in August 2007, Ted Evans and his board appointed a woman to be the CEO of the Group – the first such appointment for a major bank in Australia.

At this point, 'glacial' was the word being used to describe the pace at which women were advancing into senior leadership in corporate Australia, and it was the right word. A 2008 census revealed that women held only 8.3 per cent of board directorships and only 10.7 per cent of executive management positions. In addition, Australia was lagging behind other industrialised countries. The call for substantial change was loud and strong. Like it or not, Australian corporates needed to get on board. The issue was now urgent.

My start date at Westpac was 1 February 2008, and I immediately set about seeking to understand the culture of the bank. The first few weeks confirmed to me the strength of its focus on diversity, and my early thoughts were: Great. This is something I won't have to worry about – we have this in hand. That proved to be wrong. Within 18 months, it was clear that progress on increasing the number of women in management had stalled. I started to receive direct and indirect comments suggesting that the diversity agenda did not have my support, and our August 2009 culture audit confirmed these messages. I was stung by the feedback. Diversity was something I knew I understood. It was very important to me. Clearly I was not showing this in my leadership within Westpac. The

---

41   In introducing paid parental leave within Westpac, Ann Sherry was a pioneer. This was another 'first' within corporate Australia. Within two years, virtually every major company had decided to follow.

fact that I had an almost overwhelming set of agenda items on my plate was no excuse: I had dropped the ball, and it was hurting me.

I was fortunate to have alongside me an outstanding chief of staff, Rebecca Lim (now general counsel for the Group). Her comment to me was that the situation was readily rectifiable but that I needed to move quickly. Together we designed a set of immediate next steps:

- I met individually and collectively with a wide range of senior women across the Group to request their input and support. I received excellent advice to which I listened closely.
- In providing feedback to the organisation on the culture audit results, I explicitly addressed the importance of diversity. I stated that the agenda had my wholehearted support, and that it was something I would champion.
- I requested work be done on establishing a set of targets for women in management, and '35 per cent by 2014' came back as the recommendation. 'Too soft – not stretching enough' was my comment. With no science to it, I declared that 40 per cent women in management by 2014 would be our goal. I communicated this target internally and externally as strongly as I could.
- I engaged with the board and with individual directors. I found Carolyn Hewson's[42] counsel to be particularly valuable.

Within weeks, a comprehensive diversity strategy had been finalised and was in execution. The 'hard-wiring' elements included: a Diversity Council chaired by me with the full Group Executive team

---

42   Carolyn Hewson is one of Australia's most distinguished and influential directors. She served on the Westpac Board from 2003 to 2012.

as its members; locking in a series of targets to support and enable our 2014 goal of 40 per cent women in management; ensuring that measures were reflected in scoreboards, starting with mine at board level; tracking and measuring female progression and reviewing pipelines at our half-yearly 'People Days'; specific and individually tailored action plans; conducting a biennial diversity and flexibility survey; innovative plans targeting recruitment and development such as our 'Women in Technology' program and, in 2014, Brian Hartzer's 'Equilibrium' program, aimed at mid-management women who had been identified as great leaders in other sectors.

The 'soft-wiring' elements were equally important. They included: active and public communication of our commitment and our targets; consistent and regular communication internally of why this mattered, how we were setting about it and the progress being made; leaders role-modelling expected behaviours and explicitly calling out those that were unacceptable; regular informal lunches known as 'brown-paper-bag lunches' where we discussed issues, blockages and opportunities; recognising and celebrating progress; actively contributing to community events such as International Women's Day and the National Breast Cancer Foundation's Awareness Week; and, together with the *Australian Financial Review*, designing and managing the annual '100 Women of Influence' awards.

To assist us with the program we appointed a talented executive, Rachel Slade. Rachel was fantastic. When I asked her how she was dealing with people resistant to change or slow to come on board, she said, 'I explain what we are doing and why. I ask them to get on the bus. I then tell them the bus is leaving and it's leaving now, so if you don't get on board, you are going to be left behind.' Her energy, her drive, her clarity of why this mattered were outstanding.

The end result? We achieved our 40 per cent women in management goal two years ahead of target, and shortly thereafter I publicly communicated a new goal of 50 per cent women in management by end 2017, the year of our 200th anniversary. I announced this aspirational target at a lunch in Sydney, and I remember the look on the faces of my team. It was not something we had discussed or modelled; it was simply the obvious next thing to do. I knew I would have no problem with the team being on board.

Flexibility at work was a further important element of our strategy. There are a number of factors that make it difficult for women to progress in their careers. One of these is the typical inflexibility of a company to design work to better suit individuals and their particular needs. Fixed schedules of long hours where employees are required to be at the office, coupled with subtle and sometimes not-so-subtle pressure to regularly be available beyond normal hours, make it very hard to achieve balance in life – to be a wife, a mother, a career woman, and to be effective in all these roles.

I was fortunate in my years in South Africa to have an employer who enabled me to build flexibility into my work life. I worked part-time for two and a half years after our first child, Sharon, was born. I returned to work 12 months after the birth of Sean, Mark and Annie and was expressly told that I had the freedom to tackle the general-management job in any way that worked best for me. It was fortunate that I lived near where I worked, and very helpful, too, that the bank established a childcare centre on our work premises. 'Gym or childcare centre?' had been the discussion among the executive team, and my appointment as General Manager, Human Resources sealed the debate. A childcare centre it would be. There is no doubt that Nedcor Bank was well ahead of its time.

I felt supported and empowered to achieve a reasonable degree of balance.

Christine Parker, our group executive for human resources, has led the Westpac charge on this issue. Christine is a passionate advocate for diversity in the workplace. She is also the best HR executive that I have worked with. Her goal was to 'mainstream' flexibility, to make it the way work got done. Technology helps greatly, as it is easy to work anywhere and be connected. In addition, societal norms are changing – younger generations will not readily sign up for the '9 to 5' working arrangements older generations grew up with. Mainstreaming flexibility means mainstreaming for men *and* women. In our diversity survey of 2010 we learned that 43 per cent of our people were working flexibly in some way, and this increased to 74 per cent in 2016. We used this feedback as impetus to redesign jobs and office space. Under the direction of our chief operating officer, John Arthur, the bank's new Sydney offices at Barangaroo and our Melbourne office in Collins Street now reflect new ways of working and collaborating. The revolution is underway, yet in an overall sense it seems to me that Australian businesses still have a long way to go.

Additionally, over this period we broadened the definition of diversity. While our focus on gender was always top of mind, we initiated strategies and employee action groups across a number of other important areas:

- mature-aged workers, with the action group name being 'Prime of Life';
- our young people – 'The Youth Network';
- workers with disability or accessibility requirements – 'Assisting Better Lives for Everyone';

- Indigenous employees – 'Brothers and Sisters';
- lesbian, gay, bisexual, transgender and intersex (LGBTI) employees – 'GLOBAL';
- supporting staff and families experiencing violence in the home – 'Anti-Family Violence'; and
- improving Asian culture awareness – 'Asian Leadership'.

A Group Executive team member sponsored each of these groups, and provided regular feedback at our Diversity Council. I am particularly proud of the Reconciliation Action Plans (RAP) we developed for Indigenous employees, communities and customers. These plans built on the bank's longstanding engagement in the area and embodied important initiatives with respect to employment, supporting the growth of Indigenous Australian businesses, financial inclusion and advocacy.[43] In Cape York, for example, around 800 Westpac secondees have lived and worked with Indigenous leaders, teachers and small business proprietors, bringing not only their energy and enthusiasm, but also their business experience and skills. The goal: capacity building at a local level, seeking to facilitate economic development through targeted assistance. Our secondees found the experience extremely powerful. They learned what it is like to live for a concentrated period (typically six weeks) in a remote community. They brought back and further infused within the company a deep appreciation and respect for the culture and traditions of Indigenous Australians.[44]

---

43 Our third RAP launched in 2014 was awarded the highest 'Elevate' status by governing body Reconciliation Australia.
44 The Cape York program commenced in 2001 and was developed in partnership with Jawun Indigenous Corporate Partnerships. The force behind this powerful program was Ann Sherry. On the back of a visit by Ted Evans and myself in 2009, we extended the program to communities in Redfern and Waterloo in inner Sydney, enabling more employees to participate in secondments and longer-term mentoring.

Westpac employees are proud to celebrate difference, and they are increasingly willing to advocate for it.

Perhaps as a consequence, there was never much pushback on the 'Why are we doing this?' question. The business case for a more diverse and inclusive culture was self-evident. Our strategies gained traction and the results followed. Not only did we exceed our diversity targets, but our bottom-line performance strengthened too. Employee engagement achieved its highest level ever – 87 per cent, with 91 per cent saying they were proud to work for the Westpac Group. Globally, Westpac continued to receive recognition. In January 2014, the bank was named as the World's Most Sustainable Company at the World Economic Forum in Davos, Switzerland. Later that year, it was announced as the leading bank in the Dow Jones Sustainability Indices Review.

In summary, generosity of spirit and valuing diversity go hand in hand. What if, in our world of conflict and division, we had a lot more of each? The lesson for me as a leader and as a human being is that I can get better at both. I can open my eyes and extend my hand. I can listen and I can learn. I can build bridges of understanding. I can offer help, and I can welcome receiving it.

In 1995 I spent four weeks at INSEAD, one of the world's leading business schools. A professor in organisational development had this to say:

'Treating her as you would like to be treated is good. Even better, try treating her as she would like to be treated.'

I like that.

8
_____

GOOD WITH CHANGE

My comfort with change and ambiguity is partly due to my strongly practical nature. My years in business in South Africa during the late 1980s and the 1990s also left their mark. We lived through uncertain times in a country undergoing major change. If you couldn't adapt, you were going to be left behind. The fluidity in the system was remarkable; being prepared to step up and take responsibility meant you could accomplish a lot. You would certainly make mistakes, but you would be expected to learn from them.

One of the cultural elements I struggled with when I arrived at the Commonwealth Bank of Australia was its strong process orientation. There were lots of rules, red tape, forms, approvals, people who could say no; lots of committees, meetings, pre-meetings, briefing papers before and after. It was difficult to get things done. And when decisions *were* made, fence-sitting, spreading the risk, preparing for the downside, and later revision of the facts were common behaviours.

Years later, at Westpac, I encountered this again – a high level of bureaucracy, and stifling rules. Changing this was much harder than I expected. When I expressed frustration at the blocking mechanisms to be found everywhere, a recommendation came back proposing that we form a committee to bust bureaucracy!

At around the same time, I was also keen to change the way customer complaints were handled. How customers are managed in the complaint process is a great litmus test for just how customer-centric an organisation truly is. I discovered that customer complaints were processed by a central unit according to very strict and inflexible protocols. All letters started the same way, 'With reference to your complaint . . .', and concluded with words to the effect of 'If you are not happy, please feel free to contact the ombudsman'. The letters were sent without signature, under the general and anonymous descriptor 'Manager'.

I proposed a few simple changes:

- Personalise the letter and include the customer-service officer's name, email and telephone number.
- Tailor the response to meet the customer's concerns. Avoid stock-standard opening sentences, and avoid 'bank-speak'. In other words, communicate in a clear, direct, understandable way.

- Reply quickly to acknowledge receipt of the customer's letter, even if more time is required to investigate the issue.
- Apologise when necessary, especially for the inconvenience that the customer has experienced. Don't hesitate to express empathy and concern.
- Go the extra mile to fix things.
- Be prepared to telephone the customer to listen, to acknowledge, and then outline the next steps. In my experience, this usually takes the heat out of the situation and increases understanding on both sides.
- Wherever it makes sense to do so, involve the relevant regional manager and/or bank manager. Apart from being empowering, a local follow-up helps in closing off the issue. It also often leads to further business.
- Make sure we measure the right things. Simply writing a letter to the customer does not mean the matter is closed.
- Identify the underlying systemic issues and elevate them.
- Insist that senior line managers review the complaints relevant to their areas. This is something I personally prioritised. I found it extremely valuable in better understanding customer pain points.

I really battled to have these commonsense changes embedded. I encountered lots of 'Yes, Minister' behaviour, with the team hoping my attention would move on to other things and their lives could return to normal. When this didn't happen and I kept at it, it was suggested that these changes would put the bank at risk from a legal point of view; our current processes were designed to protect us. Well, of course that got me going again. In frustration, I called

Allan and me, April 1975. We were halfway through the Otter Trail, a magnificent five-day hike along the Garden Route of the Cape Coast.

My father, Herby Currer, poses in his Springbok jersey, 1933. He was first selected to play for South Africa at the age of sixteen.

My mother, Patricia Pettigrew, before she was married. The youngest of her siblings, she was known for her free spirit.

My mother and father with my brother Trevor and me. This photo was taken in the garden of our Waterkloof home in Pretoria in 1959.

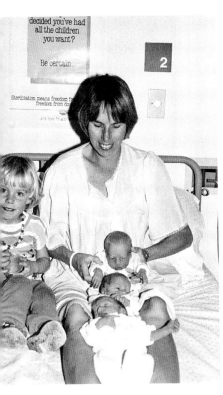

ABOVE LEFT: With my three-year-old daughter Sharon, and our newborn triplets – Sean, Mark and Annie – in 1989. The poster above my bed in the Johannesburg General Hospital posed the question: *'Have you decided you've had all the children you want?'*

ABOVE RIGHT: The babies – quite an armful!

BELOW: Three blond heads, Mark, Annie and Sean, around five years old.

LEFT: The St.George Bank half-year financial results presentation, May 200[...] Happy Dragon was there to welcome analysts, investors and media.
News Corp / Newspix

BELOW: 17 August 2007, the day of my appointment as CEO of Westpac. At th[...] media conference with our chairman, T[...] Evans, and the outgoing CEO, David Morgan. *News Corp / Newspix*

st as sustainability has moved to the centre of the business agenda,
e have placed customers at the heart of our sustainability priorities."
Kelly

With my chairman,
Ted Evans, at our
head-office building
in Kent Street, Sydney.
Ted was a strong
advocate for our
customer-centred
strategy.
Westpac Group

Westpac's merger
with St.George in 2008
was transformational
for the Group.
Westpac Group;
News Corp / Newspix

Following the merger with St.George, the Westpac Group had:

10M	1,200	2,700	25%	$108B
CUSTOMERS	BRANCHES	AUTOMATIC TELLER MACHINES	SHARE OF THE HOME LOANS MARKET	FUNDS UNDER ADMINISTRATION

'The customer-focused cultures of both St.George and Westpac are fundamental to
this merger. By bringing the two banks together we will create Australia's leading
financial institution, one that is driven to deliver for its customers.'

Gail Kelly

ABOVE: My brother Trevor and me with our mother at my niece
Rachel's wedding in 2010. Mum died later that year.

BELOW: Closing bell for the New York Stock Exchange on 16 November 2010.
My son Mark is immediately to my right, with Rob Whitfield, CEO of the Institutional
Bank, and Andrew Bowden, our head of investor relations, to my left.

6. Indra Nooyi
CEO,
PEPSICO,
U.S. AGE: 54

This year Nooyi nudged a $20 million slice of the company's $616-million-a-year ad budget away from traditional outlets to social media. A worldwide campaign, Pepsi Refresh, lets you submit grant proposals to a website, then encourages online voters to choose the winners (amounts: $5,000 to $250,000). "It blurs the line between philanthropy and advertising," says Nooyi. Refresh also allocates $1.3 million each month for a U.S. project, such as the recent "Do Good for the Gulf," which offers stipends to build a shelter for animals whose owners lost their homes to the oil spill and to provide mental health services and job training. "Brands have to speak to millenniums; young people want to make a difference," she says.

FAST FACTS:
• Annual compensation package last year was $14.2 million
• Every 2 weeks e-mails 285,000 staffers about what's on her mind

4. Angela Merkel
CHANCELLOR, GERMANY
AGE: 56

She has helped steer Germany's economy through the worst, pointing the way for the rest of the EU. Merkel also knows how to handle a fragile coalition, as she tries to push through education and tax reforms before next spring's regional elections. With business sentiment near alltime highs, she can spend some of that political capital. Germany's planned 4% cuts in the 2011 budget ($400 billion) may anger constituents, many of whom are looking for wage raises.

7. Lady Gaga
SINGER, ENTERTAINER, U.S.
AGE: 24

Born Stefani Germanotta, Lady Gaga has reinvigorated pop music. Her first album, The Fame, debuted in 2008, scoring 2 No. 1 hits with "Just Dance" and "Poker Face." She's now on a par with Beyoncé, Rhianna and Mariah Carey for the most No. 1 hits (6) by a female artist. Her Monster's Ball tour is poised to gross $200 million by the time it ends in April 2011.

8. Gail Kelly
CEO, WESTPAC, AUSTRALIA
AGE: 54

She's the head of the second-largest bank in Australia, with $551 billion in assets and $27.5 billion in revenue in the last year.

FAST FACTS:
• Mother of 4; started career as teacher

5. Hillary Rodham Clinton

SECRETARY OF STATE, U.S. AGE: 62

Diplomatic breakthroughs are rare. And while Clinton, a former First Lady and senator, brings star power to the State Department, she has yet to score a triumph beyond "resetting" the button in U.S.-Russian ties and the Turkey-Armenia treaty. She has put her skills on the line with an umpteenth attempt to broker Middle East peace, still a near impossible dream. Critics point to a lack of vision for American power but credit her close relationship with Defense Secretary Robert Gates (she prevailed over the Vice President to send 20,000 extra troops to Afghanistan last year). No one discounts her continuing contributions to the plight of women worldwide: victims of rape in Congo and flooding in Pakistan; the millions of mothers exposed to dangerous cookstoves. What's next for Hillary? Heading up the World Bank—or becoming Obama's running mate in 2012?

FAST FACTS:
• Has logged 332,156 miles traveling on diplomatic missions as of mid-September
• Has notched series of firsts for a former First Lady: running for public office (twice); becoming female senator from New York; being named to a Cabinet post

9. Beyoncé Knowles
SINGER AND FASHION
DESIGNER, U.S. AGE: 29

FAST FACTS:
• Songs are on Michelle Obama's iPod
• Keeps photo of an Academy Award near her treadmill for inspiration
• First female artist to win 6 Grammy awards in one year

10. Ellen DeGeneres
TALK SHOW HOST, U.S. AGE: 52

FAST FACTS:
• Now in eighth season, her show is seen by an average of 3 million viewers a day
• Brought national attention to a gay teenager who challenged her school's policy banning same-sex prom dates
• Is the face of Vitaminwater Zero and Cover Girl's antiaging cosmetics
• Wife, Portia de Rossi, took DeGeneres' name last month
• Has 5 million-plus Twitter followers

This 2010 Forbes List of the 100 Most Powerful Women caused much hilarity in the Kelly household. My daughters, who are fans of both Lady Gaga and Beyoncé, could not comprehend the position of their mother, sandwiched between the two.

Representing Westpac at the January 2011 Senate inquiry with Group Executive colleagues, Peter Hanlon and Phil Coffey. *Sasha Woolley/Fairfax Syndication*

On 10 March 2011, the Bank of Melbourne was re-launched. On the podium is the new bank's first CI Scott Tanner, with Ted Baillieu, former premier of Victoria, to his left. *Wayne Taylor/Fairfax Syndicati*

All in pink with my daughter Annie; we were raising awareness and providing
support for the wonderful work of the National Breast Cancer Foundation.
Brendon Thorne/Getty Images

On a field trip to Malawi as CARE Australia's ambassador for women's empowerment.
With me is Julia Newton-Howes, former CEO of CARE Australia, my daughter Sharon and
children from a rural community. © *Josh Estey/CARE*

On 21 June 2012, I participated in the St Vincent de Paul Society's CEO Sleepout, an important annual event to raise money for the homeless. *News Corp / Newspix*

Unveiling of the Nelson Mandela bust at the University of New South Wales in 2013. I was honoured to be asked to deliver the Wallace Wurth Lecture on this special occasion. With me is the former South African high commissioner to Australia, Ms. Koleka Mqulwana, and the University's former vice-chancellor, Professor Fred Hilmer. *Andy Baker / © 2013 The University of New South Wales (UNSW Sydney)*

One of my proudest days as Westpac CEO was 2 April 2014, the day we launched the bank's $100 million Bicentennial Foundation. By means of this foundation, 100 Australians will receive educational grants every year, forever. The attendance of so many children from a wide variety of schools made this launch day particularly special for me. *News Corp / Newspix*

November 2014, the University of Sydney conferred honorary doctorates on a number of Australian women who have made a difference in their respective fields. From left to right, they were: Gillian Armstrong, Dr Kerry Schott, myself, Catherine Livingstone, Elizabeth Broderick and Justice Virginia Bell. Standing on either side of the group is Belinda Hutchinson, chancellor of the University, and Dr Michael Spence, vice-chancellor. *Sarah Rhodes/The University of Sydney*

Meeting with fellow banking CEOs in Washington DC in October 2014. On my left is James Gorman, chairman and CEO of Morgan Stanley, in front of me is Jamie Dimon, chairman and CEO of JPMorgan Chase & Co, and to my right is Anshu Jain, the then co-CEO of Deutsche Bank. *Peter Stepanek Photography Washington DC*

The Global Board of Advisors at the Council on Foreign Relations, a non-profit think tank specialising in US foreign policy and international affairs. Richard Haass, first on the left in the standing row, is the president and David Rubenstein, sitting directly in front of me, is chairman of the global advisory body. This photo was taken at our 2015 annual meeting. *Ivan Villegas/Council on Foreign Relations*

LEFT: In November 2014, the G20 was hosted by Australia in Brisbane. As one of the business leaders at the forum, I had the opportunity to meet many of the G20 leaders. Here I am introduced to President Obama by Mike Baird, former premier of New South Wales.
Rob Maccoll

BELOW: With Westpac chairman, Lindsay Maxsted, and newly appointed CEO, Brian Hartzer, on 13 November 2014, the day I announced my retirement.
News Corp / Newspix

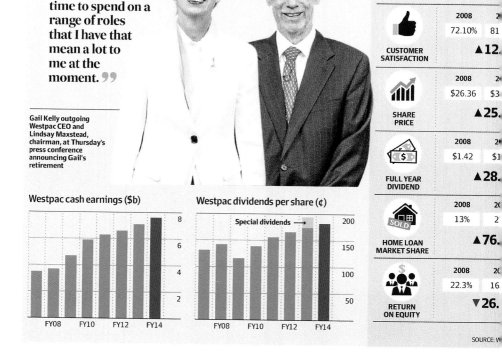

The *Australian Financial Review* printed this high-level scorecard the day after I announced my retirement from Westpac. I am standing alongside the bank's chairman, Lindsay Maxsted. *Fairfax Syndication*

My daughter Sharon presenting me with a gift from the family at my farewell dinner in 2015. The gift reflects my love affair with Africa and its wildlife. *Tim Swallow*

On the occasion of Westpac's Bicentennial in April 2017, the current and former CEOs engaged in a panel discussion with employees. From left to right: Bob White (1977–87), Frank Conroy (1991–92), Bob Joss (1993–99), David Morgan (1999–2008), myself (2008–15) and Brian Hartzer (2015–). *Mediakoo/HiredGun*

Westpac is recognised for its groundbreaking contribution in promoting gender equality and the advancement of women in management. From left to right: Judy Scott (first female full-time teller in Australian banking), me (first female major bank CEO in Australia), Helen Lynch (first female bank manager in Australia) and Ann Sherry (first to introduce paid parental leave for corporates). *Mediakoo/HiredGun*

The family at our Terrey Hills home in Sydney, 2017. From left: Sharon, English teacher, Mark, mechanical engineer, Annie, marketing executive, Sean, medical doctor, Allan and me.

Allan and me on Lake Kariba in Zimbabwe, midway through our 3½ month African adventure after retiring from Westpac.

in my Group Executive colleague, Peter Hanlon. After months of me making no progress, he redesigned and fixed things relatively quickly. The tried and tested change-management techniques were put into practice: communicate clearly what the change is and why it is necessary, then ensure that people have the skills and capabilities to make the change. Under Peter's leadership, new protocols were established, measurements and key success factors were adjusted, and lots of recognition, support and coaching were provided. Peter actively monitored the change process and stayed with it throughout. For me it was a relief, and a fresh reminder that driving internal change is hard. If you want it to stick, you have to do more than simply tell people what you want.

Driving internal change is one thing – responding to complex, simultaneous external challenges is quite another. In the aftermath of the global financial crisis, bankers found themselves having to do just this. A set of major new factors came into play.

- Change force number one: the economic slowdown coupled with a low interest-rate environment. Growth becomes much harder to achieve. Productivity is the new watchword. Business models need to change.

- Change force number two: the 'new rules of banking', regulatory rules that go much wider than capital, liquidity and funding. Almost every aspect of the organisation is affected, including issues of conduct, governance and the management of customer relationships. The implementation challenge is complex, expensive, time-consuming and seemingly never-ending.

- Change force number three: the 'new world of banking'. This is the most interesting force for change and in the long term the most significant. Two major technology revolutions are underway, being digital (comprising mobile, social media, cloud and big data) and automation (drones and robots, sensing technologies, artificial intelligence and the internet of things). Beyond these, quantum computing holds the promise of astonishing gains in basic computing power and speed that will create further waves of innovation. Unlike many previous technological revolutions, this one is customer-driven. Customers love the power of the new technologies that give them information, access and decision-making tools packaged in innovative and unexpected ways. The impact on banking, and almost every other industry, will be profound. Business boundaries will blur, the skills and capabilities to serve customers will shift, jobs will be redefined, innovators and disrupters will challenge incumbents. We are, I suspect, only at the beginning of what many are calling another Industrial Revolution.

A key challenge for leaders is that these forces of change frequently don't sit well together. For example, the 'new rules of banking' and the 'new world of banking' pull in different directions. New regulation and compliance requirements lead to heightened risk awareness, tighter controls and tougher sanctions when things go wrong. The room for error narrows. I have been in boardrooms where executives are required to 'please explain' a series of control breaches or a failure of compliance. These are serious and tough discussions, with directors appropriately applying their oversight role, testing for systemic failure and for issues of cultural breakdown. Responsible executives are held accountable, and depending on the seriousness of the situation, they can expect written warnings, demotion or termination. At the very least, remuneration outcomes are affected. It should not come as a surprise, therefore, that risk aversion grows.

In contrast, successfully changing and adapting to the 'new world of banking' calls for a culture of experimentation and innovation, of courage and agility. New entrants taking on the banks in critical areas such as payments are nimble and fast. They innovate from the customer perspective, keep testing and retesting, and are comfortable with failure. They think and act very differently from bankers. They are largely free from regulatory pressures and totally free from the public scrutiny bankers face.

As Westpac CEO, I thought deeply about all this:

- I was determined that we should not become stuck in the world of regulation and compliance. We would execute on that agenda, of course, and do so sustainably. But we would not allow it to sap our energy or dampen our courage.
- I was determined that we use the opportunity provided by new technologies to drive innovation and transform the customer experience. I wanted to build excitement and passion around this.
- To do all of the above, while also delivering acceptable returns in this low-growth world, called for resourcefulness and collaboration. Reduce bureaucracy, reduce waste, simplify.

That was the plan. As Brian Hartzer puts it, 'We need to operate like a 200-year-old start-up.' Yes, but how do we do that? These are some of the things we tried, some of the things we learned. Most can be generalised across industries and businesses.

1. *Putting the customer at the centre matters even more.*
   In banking, a robust and rigorous job in implementing the New Rules should result in a stronger bank and additional protection and support for the customer. It is crucial to approach implementation with the customer firmly in mind, understanding the underlying purpose of the new rules rather than viewing them exclusively through a compliance and legal lens. For example, new requirements in terms of identifying customers, the provision of advice or lending responsibly need to be designed to avoid a jarring or cumbersome customer experience. Design to make it easier, to enable and empower customers rather than to put extra steps and hurdles in their way. This is exactly the approach required to be effective in the New World of Banking. Customers have increasing choice in how they go about meeting their everyday financial needs and are simply not going to put up with processes that are clunky, inconvenient or difficult to navigate.

2. *Put a lot of effort into properly constructing a 'Risk Appetite Statement'.* This is an important piece of work, as it identifies categories of risk and aligns risk tolerances with the company's strategy. Executives understand what matters and why. From this statement, control frameworks can be developed and accountabilities established. What is 'not negotiable' becomes really clear. For example, an organisation should have 'zero tolerance' with regard to health and safety breaches, and similar zero tolerance for

breaches of financial controls or the privacy of customer information. Experimentation and adopting a trial and error approach are simply not acceptable in these areas. On the other hand, if risk-appetite work is properly done, it is immediately evident that there are many areas crying out for innovation and creativity, where people need to be encouraged to do things differently. Every product and customer process falls into this category – seek to make it easier, more transparent and in line with the customer need. In summary, discipline and creativity can coexist. In fact, more than that: the stability of disciplines and frameworks enable flexibility and creativity. They free executives up.

3. Be prepared to *challenge the longstanding implicit beliefs about the industry or about the organisation*. The banking industry has long believed that the heavy load of regulation creates a significant barrier to entry for others; it has also held the view that scale is the key to profitability. Does digitisation, combined with cloud-based computing and big data, change this? New entrants can offer discrete banking services using the new technologies at lower costs and with more direct value to customers. Peer-to-peer lending is an example. Traditionally, banks have served as the intermediaries between lenders and borrowers. Peer-to-peer lending businesses are not banks. They link people with funds to people who need funds using sophisticated algorithms. They are able to differentiate between borrowing customers in terms of their credit histories. Their fee structures reflect their simpler, more transparent operating model.

4. *Try and test new models of innovation* and use a number of them in practice. This may include partnering with start-ups and/or buying new-entrant businesses. It is also likely to involve a number of internal initiatives, such as establishing dedicated 'innovation labs', allocating specific pools of dollars for research and development (R&D) work, creating centres of excellence in digital, and appointing customer experience team members to ensure the customer is kept at the centre of the innovation. Sometimes the easiest and best way to drive change and show what is possible, and how quickly it is possible, is to establish something brand new, unencumbered by legacy. Set up the team or separate business unit and give them the mandate to redesign specific processes from scratch. Make sure they adopt a customer-centred mindset.

5. While trialling a number of initiatives has value, it does not in itself move the dial in transforming the organisation and the customer experience. *Integrating new applications into the core* is what does that. This is certainly not easy, it is expensive and it takes time. Typically it requires a service-oriented architecture and partnering with skilled technology providers. But achieving this goal represents a huge leap forward. Without it, executives run the risk of doing what is effectively a lot of dabbling and then becoming complacent about progress.

6. *Think digital first, think mobile first.* A great example in retail banking is the changing role of branches. Traditionally they have occupied centre-stage, the primary channel for customers. Innovations such as ATMs and

telephone banking typically served to augment them. The new imperative is to bring the bank to the customer wherever she may be and in the way that works best for her. A physical distribution mindset must become a digital mindset. The branch is but one channel.

7. *Use new language.* Brian did this very effectively in 2014 as we accelerated our change journey. Over a short period of time, senior executives were working with concepts such as 'the 90-day drop', 'huddles', 'the garage', 'the accelerator', 'agile' and others. Decision-making routines were changed to drive innovation.

8. Across the organisation, seek to *take out complexity and have work done differently.* How projects are managed is a good example. In many cases, they need to be smaller, tighter in their scope, and faster in their delivery timeframes. All the right people need to be co-located as the project progresses to avoid the 'waterfall approach' of business specification, translated into technical specification, translated into technical design, translated into build, user testing, acceptance testing, sign-off and the like. These various steps need to be done iteratively and in real time, with decision-makers right there. Collaboration across traditional boundaries – divisional, functional and hierarchical – is the new skill.

9. *Make sure critical innovation initiatives are resourced to succeed,* with adequate funding, the right people involved, and a top executive sponsor who is invested in the initiative's success. In my experience, a committed, customer-centred leader will set the bar high, hold the team

to account, and knock down barriers that have the potential to hamper progress.

10. *Kill things off quickly if they don't work.* This involves a simpler process for business-case development and post-implementation reviews. It involves a different attitude towards learning and towards failure.

11. *Personalise the story of the transformation.* Communicate, communicate, communicate – the what, the why, the how. As much as possible, speak in customer terms. Employees are themselves customers. They can relate to why 'knowing your customer' matters, why making it easier makes sense. They too are living their lives differently, with their smartphones ever on and with the ubiquity of social media. They understand that the world is undergoing a major set of changes because they can see and feel it in their lives. They understand that no-one knows how this will play out but that it involves material change. Ask employees to get on board. At Westpac, we added a value of 'Courage' to assist with this. It gave us the platform to discuss the behaviours we would like to see in the organisation, and gave leaders the opportunity to tell stories and to become role models.

12. *Acquire and develop new skills.* Leaders need to be more generous-spirited and collaborative. They need to listen more and empower more. Build skills across the organisation in customer-centred design, in data analysis and in creative thinking. New talent from outside the mainstream must be introduced, including young people who live and breathe the world of customer choice and

customer empowerment. To achieve this and attract the best, it is critical that the organisation has an inspiring vision and strong value proposition. The best people will seek out organisations with authentic leadership, that are hungry for transformation and change. Best people will themselves attract best people.

13. *Engage actively and often with the board.* In a bank, the board inevitably spends a lot of its time dealing with the implications and issues arising from the New Rules. It is critical that the board spends equal time in discussing and thinking through the profound implications of the New World facilitated by technology. Board members need to challenge management on whether the organisation is innovating and adapting fast enough. Do executives have the sensing mechanisms in place to understand the emerging trends? Are there sufficient executives on the team with the right skill sets?

14. *Keep top of mind the distinct strengths that the organisation has.* While the disrupter has a 'clean slate' and speed of implementation is a definite advantage, incumbent organisations have strong existing customer bases. Banks, for example, know a lot about their customers and are best placed to identify future needs and offer personalised solutions. Furthermore, banks are trusted by their customers to provide privacy, security and integrity in account information. Customers like to know that their funds and their personal details are safe. They like to know that the bank will protect them from fraud. They like to know where to go if things go wrong. These are assets

that count for a lot. Show that you can innovate too and transform the service experience, and there will be no need for a customer to leave.

In this chapter so far, I have dealt with the leadership challenges of organisational change. Let me finish with a few thoughts on personal change.

My own experience leads me to this: don't worry too much about feeling uncomfortable or uncertain. Don't pretend you are across everything that is going on. The keys to success lie in self-awareness, courage, listening skills and interpretative skills. Be prepared to make decisions and then revise them as new information comes to hand. Ensure you have the right people on board in the right roles, and back them. Recognise that dealing effectively with change requires mental toughness and resilience. In this world, things will go wrong. Mistakes will be made. The speed of change, the round-the-clock news cycle and social media will amplify these mistakes. Expect it, and get ready for it.

9

RESILIENCE

An analogy I sometimes used with my general management teams at the outset of an important program of change and expected difficulty was that of a journey. 'As we set out,' I would say, 'there is preparation we need to do. Importantly, we know exactly where we are headed; we need to recognise, however, that there is no single clear path. We will be climbing mountains, crossing valleys, navigating rivers and marshlands. We will need to find our way through dense forests. We should expect to get bogged down, to lose direction, to become tired and have differing views on what the next steps should be. We may well find ourselves under attack when we are most vulnerable. It is therefore critical that we prepare properly, that we ensure we have the right resources around us, that we are physically and mentally fit. We are a team and we will travel together. We will help each other. Even though we may need to change our plans en route, we will never lose sight of our goal.'

In using this analogy, I was looking to build resilience. I have learned that being an effective leader over a sustained period calls for an extraordinary reservoir of physical and mental strength. There is a relentlessness about fronting up each and every day to deal with the expected and the unexpected, to manage your time, your agenda and your energy, to be 'always on'. It takes planning, discipline and stamina. As the demands on me grew, I became ever-more disciplined in coping with them. It mattered that I believed in what I was doing, and that I enjoyed the challenge of leadership, of working with people and with teams. My pragmatic orientation helped, too – in tough situations, I would push hard to understand the detail of the issues we were confronting in order to determine the best pathway forward. The biggest help of all was having a positive and optimistic attitude: 'We can do this. Let's take the lessons and find the opportunities. Look how far we have come.'

Over time, and with practice, I have developed a range of mechanisms and techniques to assist me in shoring up my energy and building day-to-day resilience:

- I learned to take charge of my schedule, rather than have it defined for me. I ensured that time was explicitly set aside for reflection. This 'white space' time, as I called it, was very often drawn upon to deal with the critical issues of the day.

Setting it aside beforehand meant I had the time available. It immediately reduced the pressure.

- I prioritised having a very strong office. I found it hugely important to have people around me whom I trusted, who were themselves calm under pressure, who consistently reflected my personal tone and who were able to make decisions and advance the agenda. This gave me capacity and allowed me to perform at my best.

- I instilled the discipline of sticking to my schedule. I made sure I was on time for meetings and events, and would allow an engagement to be cancelled only if absolutely necessary. Similarly, my team knew that I was always available to them and that I would return their calls within the day. These disciplines mattered because they spoke to reliability and consistency, and to being centred even when the pressure was really on.

- I avoided making critical decisions when I was tired, stressed or energy-depleted. I did not allow myself to get into the position of being rushed. Rest and quiet thinking enhanced my judgement.

- I paced myself with regard to work-related evening and weekend commitments. They only made my schedule if I believed that my personal participation was important to my leadership role.

- I made sure my schedule had 'in the field' time – visiting branches, call centres, regional communities, teams in our head-office building. Talking to people in the business and engaging with customers at the coalface were energy-boosting activities. I would always return with a smile on my face, an extra bounce in my step, and a couple of ideas about what we could do more of, or do differently.

- I looked after my physical wellbeing by prioritising exercise, or 'fitness' as my wonderful personal assistant, Ron Pok, would call it. Walking has always been a fun activity for me. Between around 6.30 and 7.30 a.m., John Arthur, Westpac's chief operating officer, and I could often be seen striding around the Sydney Harbour foreshore. In the evenings, my son Sean and I would set out for a neighbourhood walk with our dogs. He and I have always had a fabulous relationship and our conversations never flagged. He showed no embarrassment that his mother was sometimes doing this circuit in her dressing gown!

- Ron also ensured that I ate properly. I have never been fussy about food, but healthy breakfasts and lunches became an important part of keeping me in good shape with sufficient energy for the rigours of the job.

- Sometimes, particularly in the latter part of my career, I would work from home, usually for a morning, rarely for a full day. For someone who so actively espouses flexible work practices, I should have done this more often. Why then did I find myself defensive when my son, Sean, on encountering me at our dining-room table at 10 a.m. as he emerged from his bedroom, asked, 'Why are you still here, Mum? Aren't you working today?'

- My home was, and is, a retreat for me: a place I love to be, where I can rest, read and be still. It embodies family, and the warmth and support that family brings. It is also where my five excitable, always 'very happy to see you' dogs live their lucky lives. On really tough days at work, when I feel stressed and exhausted, I hang on to the fact that I have this solid base at home that will not only replenish me but also give me perspective on the issues I am grappling with.

- Lastly, I find time for things I really enjoy. Family time and family holidays are high on the list, particularly holidays in the African bush. At home in Sydney, Allan and I love to go hiking or kayaking. Then there is reading, fiction and non-fiction, a source of real and enduring joy for me. And of course sport, almost any sport, although my favourites to follow are cricket, rugby, tennis and golf. It is certainly fortunate that I am able to get by without the need for a lot of sleep! Each in their own way, these activities help me regenerate. I mentally tune into a new mode.

My comments so far have related primarily to the resilience required for day-to-day leadership. A special type of resilience is needed for those circumstances when things have gone wrong, your back is to the wall, you have made mistakes and reputationally you and your organisation are under pressure. In late 2009, as CEO of Westpac, I found myself in this position.

On 1 December 2009, at 2.30 in the afternoon, the Reserve Bank of Australia raised the cash rate by 25 basis points to 3.75 per cent. Very soon thereafter, Westpac announced an increase to its standard variable home loan rate of 45 basis points. Our explanation for the 20 basis points over and above the Reserve Bank increase was centred on the vastly higher (approximately 10 times higher) costs of raising money we were experiencing as a direct consequence of the global financial crisis and the severe dislocation of funding markets. The rationale was a solid one, particularly as Westpac was one of only two Australian banks that had consistently continued to lend over the course of 2009. In fact, between them, Westpac and the Commonwealth Bank of Australia provided more than 80 per cent of all home finance over the year. To meet these borrowing needs, we had needed to raise money at the new elevated levels. Our costs accelerated sharply.

Notwithstanding the commercial facts, the decision was a difficult one to make. I knew we would experience a backlash and would be targeted by everyone: politicians, the media, community organisations, competitors and customers. I also knew that across all these groups there was an obsessive focus on mortgage rates. The fact that we were raising rates on certain categories of term deposits by more than 45 basis points would be largely ignored, as was the fact that we increased business lending rates by 25 basis points, in line with the Reserve Bank increase. We prepared for all this, but we prepared inadequately, and in executing the decision we made a number of mistakes. In a nutshell:

- I failed to effectively communicate with our various stakeholder groupings. As CEO, I had not done enough to simply, clearly and repeatedly articulate the implications of the global financial crisis on the banking system in Australia and on Westpac. In particular I failed to adequately explain the structural funding cost pressures confronting us in a way that the different groupings could relate to.
- I failed to personally front up on the day itself, not only to explain the decision, but also to express my understanding of its impact on customers. My chairman, Ted Evans, advised me to do so; my public relations and media team

believed my appearance would add fuel to the fire. I should have listened to my chairman. By the time I engaged, the flames were high indeed.

- I broke the basic rule of change management by making and announcing this decision at a time when a lot was going on. We did not have 'clear air' or the scope to focus on this issue alone. Around the same period, we delivered a market update presentation and implemented a Group Executive structural reorganisation. Each event provided the media with fresh material and a further opportunity to canvass old ground. By far the biggest source of new material was the 'Banana Smoothie' video, which was designed for frontline employees and was well received by them. To help explain what happens to the availability and cost of money in the event of a financial storm, the video outlined what happened to the availability and cost of bananas in the aftermath of Queensland's cyclone Larry in 2006. Once released on our website, social media erupted. The video was seen as simplistic and disrespectful. We withdrew it, but the damage was done. Media coverage was aggressive and personal.

A CEO's job is sometimes described as lonely. I typically did not find it so, but this period would be an exception. A bright spotlight was trained right on me. The accountability for the situation was mine, and the responsibility to fix it was mine too. My determination to do so formed the centrepiece of my resilience. Help came in a number of ways. I knew I had the support of my team, although many of them were stunned. Ted was unwavering.

'Correct decisions are often very unpopular' was his comment on the day of our annual general meeting later that month. Allan's infuriation with the media and the very personal nature of the commentary helped, too. I was able to say to him that this is the way it goes, it's what we should expect and we will get through it.

Within the organisation, I knew I was being closely watched. It was generally thought that I was taking the issues in my stride. I'm not sure that this was strictly true. I did, however, get out and about in the network and within our head office. At a meeting of general managers in late December, I transparently addressed the issues. I provided detailed insight into the decision itself and discussed the fallout. Team members were upset, and it was good for me to acknowledge this. I then asked for help. I indicated that we had an important job ahead of rebuilding our reputation, and asked each team member to work with me and with the executive team. Key individuals stepped up, the team was assembled, a detailed plan emerged and we set about its execution. Slowly and surely we recovered ground, and I recovered ground. I learned that being resilient is much more than having a thick skin. It's about being centred in yourself and taking responsibility. It's about being prepared to express vulnerability, to listen and learn. It's about showing you have what it takes to act and move forward.

I will finish this chapter with a brief discussion about the leader's role in assisting others. Across a team, there will be a range of ability to cope with pressure. Not everyone has inherent inner strength or resilience and, at different times for each of us, that inner strength can wax or wane. Anxiety and stress are growing phenomena in the workplace, which is perhaps not surprising in this environment of constant change and technological innovation and disruption. It is incumbent on each of us to look out for others who are struggling in order to offer support and to extend care. Small gestures, as well as listening and keeping in touch can make a big difference to the individual under stress who is feeling alone. At Westpac, we encouraged leaders to deepen personal relationships among their team members, keep watch for unusual behaviour and reach out and ask the important questions of 'How are you?' and 'What can I do to help?' Focusing on wellbeing is an important leadership role.

This point of reaching out to help others is not only a message for organisations – it is relevant for all of us in all settings, families included. Like most families, I have felt this personally. My oldest daughter went through a particularly difficult period in her mid-twenties when she experienced a long string of tough days and was feeling very low. She later shared with me the single biggest thing that helped her: every day, each of her siblings found their own way to reach out to her, to connect. Regardless of how or whether she responded, and regardless of how inadequate each may have felt in being able to help, they were there for her, and in little everyday ways showed they cared. They helped her regain her inner strength. They helped her rebuild her resilience.

ENGAGING WITH
THE MEDIA

Engaging with the media became an increasingly important part of my leadership role, but it was never something with which I felt entirely comfortable. I preferred radio to television, newspaper commentators to newspaper reporters. Social media became a phenomenon during my time as CEO of Westpac but I engaged only minimally, judging the risks to be considerable and preferring to retain as much privacy as possible.

My first experience on Australian television occurred in 2000 during my time with the Commonwealth Bank. Unusually for me, it was an interview that I wanted to give. I was annoyed about what I saw as misrepresentation and I had a message to share. My role at the time – Group Executive, Customer Service Division – involved the leadership of the 20 000-person sales and service teams for retail and business banking.

At the conclusion of each year we ran an annual recognition event, known as 'Rewarding Success', for the highest achievers across the country. The categories were diverse, including junior and senior bankers. Tellers, customer-service officers, branch managers, small business lenders, home lenders, credit officers, financial planners – all were included. Those being recognised were the best of the best, and were invited with their spouses/partners to a two-day celebration culminating in a gala dinner. Hamilton Island was that year's venue. It was a special occasion, heartwarming and motivational in equal measure. For many participants, it was their first visit to Queensland. Partners were particularly thrilled to be included and have their contributions acknowledged. Across the country, however, a wave of bank bashing was occurring, and the Commonwealth Bank was the prime target. And so it happened that Channel 9 sent a crew to Hamilton Island to gather material for *A Current Affair*. The pre-show headlines indicated that it was to be a story about greedy senior bankers rewarding themselves at a secret getaway. In its advertising, it showed pictures of people having fun, dressed for a celebration.

I was determined that this should not be a one-sided, highly negative story. I believed the extremely hardworking employees of the bank deserved better treatment, and that it was important for the truth to be told. I put my hand up to appear on the show. My CEO, David Murray, gave me excellent advice which has stuck:

'If you are going to do something like this, ensure that you do it "live". You don't want to find that much of what you have to say lands on the cutting-room floor.' David schooled me on the importance of being absolutely clear in my messages: 'Prepare and practise. Know exactly what you want to say, and make sure you say it.'

I found the experience daunting, but I was ready. I was also underestimated. Mike Munro, the *A Current Affair* journalist, was in the Melbourne studio interviewing me by video. I don't think he knew who I was or the role I fulfilled at the bank – my guess is that he thought I was in the bank's PR area and that he expected some 'spin' language. What he got was someone who came out of the blocks being very clear that she was proud of her people, saying that the award winners came from all levels of the retail and business bank and were thoroughly deserving of their recognition. If I were to look back at the interview now, I am sure I would cringe at my earnestness and combativeness. Nevertheless, I got through it okay, with my points made. I was inundated with positive messages from across the organisation, including from family members of the winners. They were pleased that the bank had stood up for them. When David played the video at the bank's board meeting, I knew I had passed a test with him, too.

My next major engagement with the media was at the time of my appointment as CEO of St.George Bank. I recall walking down the long corridor of the St.George building at Circular Quay alongside my new chairman, Frank Conroy, towards the array of journalists and cameras, thinking: Oh my goodness – am I prepared for this?

A new chapter in my corporate life had begun, and it was going to involve a considerably higher public profile. It was fortunate for me that St.George Bank was warmly regarded throughout the community. St.George was not a major bank, and had a strong customer-service culture. Although I was largely an unknown quantity, my appointment was positively received. The next six years were important ones in my career. We were able to profitably grow the bank while strengthening its customer focus and community orientation. In terms of the media, my aim was to keep as low a profile as possible. Frank advised me on this, but I didn't need much encouragement. I was concerned about the 'tall poppy' syndrome. The good run I was having and the positive coverage I received concerned me. When would the tide turn and the tall poppy be cut down? Staying under the radar and continuing to perform was the best strategy.

My appointment to the CEO position of a major bank in Australia came as less of a surprise. It had been widely reported that I was in close contention to replace David at the Commonwealth Bank when he stepped down in 2005. I was unsuccessful in that quest, with Ralph Norris being the worthy winner. Two years later, the opportunity emerged at another major bank. 'St.George's Kelly to take reins at Westpac' was the front-page headline of the *Australian Financial Review*'s early edition on 17 August 2007. Unfortunately the news had leaked out a few hours ahead of the formal announcement. It was a whirlwind of a day. Ted Evans, Westpac's chairman, hosted a media conference that involved both David Morgan, the current CEO, and me making short addresses and taking questions. I felt immensely honoured to have been chosen as the next CEO of Australia's first bank, and both Ted and David were generous in their comments. I knew that the role involved a significant step up, with a steep learning curve in store.

I also knew that I could expect a much brighter spotlight on what I did, and how I did it.

The best word to describe my engagement with the media throughout my seven years as CEO of Westpac is 'disciplined'. I prepared rigorously for formal media engagements. I tried to connect in an open and friendly way while remaining 'on message', alert to potential missteps and misinterpretations. Nevertheless, I often found myself surprised. Having given an interview on a wide range of topics, I would discover that the media article passed over what I saw as the substantive points and found an angle involving something relatively minor. I would find that I was presented as being emphatic on the identified issue.

Headlines also caused problems – some were downright misleading, while others were completely or partially disconnected from the rest of the article. An excellent example of this was the headline 'Westpac chief Gail Kelly joins carbon tax revolt', which appeared in *The Australian* on 5 May 2011. The body of the article included these words from me:

> 'A market-based mechanism is the best way to drive the innovation to new technology and new methodologies – that has been the best approach. A carbon price is one step towards an ETS [emissions trading scheme] and I think we need to remember it is only one of the solutions that you should be putting in place.'

The quote in this article is correct – it is what I said – but the headline is completely misleading. Because of the importance of the issue at the time, I appeared on Fran Kelly's ABC *Radio National*

Breakfast show the next morning to set the record straight.[45]

A further example was the headline 'Get off Gillard's back, urges Westpac chief'. What this implied was that I was telling fellow business leaders and Australians at large what to do. This was not the case. In a post-results, broad-ranging interview, I was asked how I managed relationships with government. I outlined my general approach, which involved attempting to build constructive relationships with politicians in order to deal with issues directly. I then specifically referred to the prime minister, Julia Gillard, stating that in my experience she was a consultative leader and I had found in her a refreshing preparedness to engage: 'She does listen, I can tell you from personal experience. Even if you have a different starting point she will listen. And I really respect that in politicians.' Due to the unpopularity of the Gillard Government within the business community, the article attracted a lot of attention. Despite the mischief-making headline, I stand by my remarks.

Something that surprised me when I arrived in Australia was the popularity and power of talkback radio. Although I did not engage much with the medium, I developed a constructive relationship with Alan Jones, Australia's best-known and most influential talkback radio host. It did not start well. Early in my tenure as CEO of St.George Bank, Alan wrote to me requesting bank sponsorship for a concert featuring talented young artists. I politely declined. Usually this signals the end of things. Not so with Alan, who addressed me again, letting me know that he thought my decision, for what was after all not a lot of money, was a poor one. I proposed that we meet, and some weeks later I arrived at Alan's Sydney apartment, early and

---

45   Westpac's position is one that accepts the scientific evidence that climate change is real and affects communities. Among other things, Westpac advocates for market mechanisms on carbon pricing to incentivise businesses to drive innovation and change.

on my guard. Fifteen minutes later, he burst in with his characteristic energy and we immediately sat down to lunch.

I'm not quite sure how it happened, but in no time at all we locked on to an area of mutual love: the world of sport. Alan found in me a fellow devotee, someone who in her growing-up years had spent Saturday after Saturday, Sunday after Sunday at sporting venues in and around Pretoria. This was a person who at 13 years of age had accompanied the Under 15 Northern Transvaal Cricket Team on their tour of Rhodesia. Her father was coach and manager, her brother was captain and she had an official role as the team scorer, sitting in the stands watching every ball, scorebook in lap and pencil in hand. At this harbour-side lunch, it was mainly cricket we discussed – the 1960s, '70s, '80s and '90s through to the current day. The players, the teams, the politics. Almost without pausing for breath, an hour and a half became two. Looking at our watches, we stood up and hastily said our goodbyes.

A relationship had formed and every couple of months or so, I would receive a letter from Alan asking me to look into a particular customer matter. Each time I wrote back, usually a handwritten letter, to thank him and assure him that the matter had my personal oversight.[46] The practice continued into my Westpac years where, due to the financial crisis, the customer matters generally became more complex, requiring negotiation and discussion, and weeks rather than days to find acceptable solutions. Find them, however, we did. Without even realising it, Alan and I had hit upon a further area of common interest: a passion for helping people experiencing difficulties. Our model of engagement worked for all involved.

As discussed in the 'Resilience' chapter, one of the most

---

46   While I had help dealing with them, all customer letters written to me had my personal oversight.

significant tests of my leadership occurred in the aftermath of our 45 basis points increase in mortgage rates. While the decision we made was always going to be unpopular, we made it worse for ourselves in a number of ways, including through inadequate communication and poor execution. What followed was a period of sustained negative publicity. Conventional media, talkback radio and social media all threw their weight into this story, and I was at the centre of the storm. When the initial phase died down, the hunt was on for fresh and personal angles. Camera crews set up outside my home, my private financial affairs were inexpertly trawled over, and comments from mostly anonymous third parties were sought.

I absorbed the pressure, remained consistent in my behaviour and demeanour, and waited it out. The work of reputation rebuilding then began. Some, including brand-management experts, voiced doubts about whether rebuilding was possible. But they reckoned against the strength and commitment of the board and management team, and our determination to execute on the Group's sustainability agenda. The years 2010 to 2012 were tough. We went back to basics, defined our purpose and doubled down on our customer-centred strategy. From 2013 we hit our straps on delivery, producing our highest-ever employee engagement score. In 2014, for the first time in a long time, Westpac and St.George pulled ahead of major bank peers in consumer and business satisfaction. Our ROE of 16.4 per cent was a full percentage point higher than it had been in 2012. We regained the position of global industry leader in the Dow Jones Sustainability Indices Review. When I rang the chairman, Lindsay Maxsted, to pass on this news, he commented: 'That's a lot of people, doing a lot of right things, over a long period of time.' Steady focus, clarity of purpose and disciplined execution produced these outcomes. The media came with us on the journey, and our 2014 results were positively reported.

As I stated at the outset of this chapter, however, engaging with the media has always been something of a challenge for me. My performance can best be described as mixed. Here is what worked for me:

- Consistency of approach: always polite, professional and engaging.
- Being disciplined, 'on message' and preparing thoroughly. This included avoiding 'throwaway lines' or taking pot shots at others.
- Willingness to take responsibility, having a thick skin and not overreacting.
- Being comfortable to talk about myself as well as the business I was leading. I understood the natural interest in my gender, my family and 'how I coped with it all'. I handled these questions without impatience or frustration.
- Choosing platforms of schools, universities, charities and customer events for my external speeches. I was able to communicate important messages on themes of leadership, change, customer-centricity and the economic outlook, with low levels of media attention.
- Understanding that, above all else, high-quality delivery of the strategic agenda matters.

If I had my time as CEO again, these are things I would do differently:

- Build stronger personal relationships with individual journalists and with editors. You are more likely to be fairly reflected if you are better understood. This was a direct learning from the December 2009 event.

- Ensure that the organisation has a strong, highly skilled and experienced media relations team (and government relations team, for that matter). Having sound relationships with all forms of media is crucial for effective backgrounding and dealing with difficult issues. Again, this was a direct learning for me from December 2009. I was sorely in need of the fearless advice and counsel a trusted Group Affairs team can bring. In later years, Carolyn McCann brought exactly that, together with deep personal care for the welfare of the organisation and its leaders.

- Be bolder and braver myself, and less concerned about making a mistake. It was sometimes remarked that I was 'overly scripted'. That is a fair comment. I should have backed myself to be more expansive while remaining 'on message'.

- Make myself more available to be the key spokesperson for the bank or for the industry on substantive matters. Again, this 'putting myself out there' was not my natural preference. On the occasions that I took on the role of chairing or participating in panel discussions, or tackling keynote interviews, it always went well. Why did I not do more?

- Excel at social media. While the risks are obvious, the opportunities are powerful. I love that through these new collaborative communication platforms, leaders can bypass traditional channels and initiate and redistribute content. They can engage directly with customers and key influencers. To be excellent at social media requires being authentic and creative. You need to be comfortable with ambiguity and with not being in control. For leaders of today, these skills are indispensable.

I will finish with what I believe to be most important of all: we worry too much about what others think of us. I know I do. My father used to tell me that what mattered most was what I thought of myself.

How do I feel about my behaviour? When I look in the mirror, do I feel comfortable with what I see? Do I pass my own high tests of character? If you answer these questions in the affirmative, you can stand tall. You can take on whatever comes your way.

PART III

LIVE A WHOLE LIFE

I

FAMILY – THE MOST IMPORTANT THING

In mid-1995, I attended the four-week INSEAD Advanced Management Program. It was great fun living on campus in Fontainebleau outside Paris and engaging with fellow business executives from around the world. The highlight of the program was the focus on leadership. The business school brought a holistic approach to this, and students were required to reflect on all elements of their lives, including their personal health and their relationships with family and friends. In terms of living a whole life, how were we performing?

Several among us felt confronted and challenged. More than one broke down. I recall a highly successful senior executive of a large European company in tears as he came to the realisation of what had happened to him, of where he stood in the overall context of his life. He may have been at the peak of his business career, but was he happy? His marriage had long since broken down and his relationship with his two sons was distant. He had not been around for their growing-up years, and they were now adults engaged in their own lives. He realised, perhaps for the first time, that his sense of self-worth was driven by what he did, rather than by who he was. He had always put his work first – he was doing it to support the family, after all. But now, as he confronted a work-life coming to an end, his family was no longer there. Indeed, what was there? His sadness was overwhelming.

I returned home from that experience determined never to find myself in that situation. I knew I too had a tendency to prioritise work, with a view that my family would always be there. I felt guilty about this, but I was driven, I was conscientious, and I didn't want to let my work colleagues down. Coming back from INSEAD, I decided to explicitly put family first.

I have no doubt that this contributed to the decision Allan and I made in April 1997 to leave South Africa. It was the toughest decision of our lives. Both of us were performing well in our respective careers, loving what we were doing and dedicated to making a difference. In Allan's case, as a paediatrician working in Baragwanath Hospital (the largest hospital in the Southern Hemisphere, based in Soweto), he was making everyday, practical and real differences to the lives of the people he helped. In addition to his work as a consultant at the hospital, he had established a paediatric HIV clinic.

He also brought a special focus to children suffering abuse. Allan's first degree had qualified him as a social worker and so he brought a holistic approach to assist his young patients and their families.

To decide to leave the country we loved was very, very difficult. The driver for the decision was our view of what was best for our family and our children. We were concerned about the long-term future of South Africa and worried about our children's safety and security – we wanted to ensure that they had opportunities for successful careers in any area they chose. I was 40, Allan was 41, and the children were still in primary school. We decided that now was the best time for the family to leave and to start new lives in a new country.

As I have reflected elsewhere, those first three to four years in Australia were extremely challenging. Nothing prepares you for the physical and emotional upheaval of a major move such as this. But like many things in life, when you emerge from difficult times, you are stronger. Certainly for us, our family unit of six became even more tight-knit. We relied upon each other for support and encouragement and looked to spend as much time as possible together. We had shared experiences and histories and were unified in our intent to forge happy and successful lives in our new home country. Each of us recognised the importance of family to our happiness.

Over the period of my working years, I have become more and more of an advocate for change in organisations – the kind of change that will allow employees to better manage and balance the different priorities in their lives. Simultaneously, I have become an advocate for higher levels of trust and openness. I recognise that I was unusually supported in my years at Nedcor Bank. When I returned to work on a part-time basis after the birth of our first child, Sharon, I was given assignments that would allow me to dictate my own schedule. I was being measured on output.

Two and a half years later, when I knew we had triplets on the way, I resigned from work, wanting to put all my focus on the priorities at hand, priorities that filled me with trepidation. Finding out about the triplets had been a shock. Fortunately I completed nearly 37 weeks in the pregnancy. All three babies, healthy and of a good size, came home with me when I left the Johannesburg General Hospital on the fourth day after their birth. Five months later, Nedcor again came calling – would I consider the role of General Manager, Human Resources? The idea seemed almost laughable at first. Even as I took the phone call, I could hear the babies crying in the background.

But on the basis of Allan's encouragement ('You'll never know unless you try'), I set off for the interview with two of the babies in tow. One I left with the receptionist and the other I took with me into the interview. I'm not sure what Peter Hibbitt, senior executive at the Perm, thought about this. If they appointed me, they would have to help me succeed. We agreed on a start date of 1 December 1990, when the triplets would be 12 months old. 'Design your day around what works for you' was the message, and 'Don't feel compelled to fit into an 8 to 5 schedule.' It is a wonderful feeling to know that you are being trusted and supported to make it work. The reality is I didn't take up the freedom to specifically tailor the role to meet my circumstances, as I was too much of a conformist at heart and didn't want to stand out from others. I can manage this, I thought. But I felt powerfully supported and that is what I most remember. Since coming to Australia, I have been determined to provide similar support to others.

Here is a small example from early in my career at St.George. On a visit to the call centre in Parramatta, I asked the leadership team about the relatively high levels of absenteeism and employee turnover in their business.

'Well, take next week,' I was told. 'It's the first week of school, so we can expect a high level of absenteeism.'

'Why should that be?' I asked.

'Mums and dads want to take their children to school and so they stay away.'

'Why don't we tackle it differently?' I suggested. 'How about addressing the topic directly with employees? Let them know that it is okay. Ask who will be needing time to take their children to school. When are they likely to arrive? Then ask if there are others who will be happy to adjust their shifts to cover this period.' In essence, I was saying, 'Why don't we encourage openness and transparency? Why don't we recognise that it is a good thing that mums and dads want to be part of this special time for their child? Why don't we explicitly prepare for this? Surely this is better than having a spike in "sick days".'

At both St.George and Westpac, we introduced a range of new policies seeking to encourage the living of 'a whole life' approach, making possible and then encouraging study-leave breaks; extending paid parental leave to 13 weeks, with the opportunity to take up to two years; providing grandparental leave; establishing onsite childcare centres at a number of our major sites; offering transition-to-retirement support; offering domestic violence support; and maintaining superannuation contributions over the parental-leave period. At the workplace itself, a variety of services were offered to enhance wellbeing, including free counselling services, priority access to specialist practitioners, free nutrition advice, and financial-planning advice.

With regard to jobs themselves, a revolution is occurring in flexible design. Who would have thought a decade ago that job-sharing could take place at the trading desks in the Institutional Bank? That call-centre employees working from home would be more productive and more engaged than those at the centre itself? That men would increasingly ask for flexible arrangements to enable them to spend more time with their children? That working where and when it makes sense would start to become the mainstream? That employees would be encouraged to have conversations about how to best balance all the priorities in their lives?

A decade ago, you would not have heard a CEO explicitly state that family is the most important priority. I am a case in point. Although I have always tried to role-model the importance of living a whole life by being comfortable talking about my husband and children, by prioritising family events and making it known I have done so, I did not actually say 'Family is the most important priority' until well into my time as CEO of Westpac. One of the triggers for being upfront on this was my mother's death in December 2010.

Mum was 93 when she died. At 80 years of age she had accompanied us on the move to Australia. Leaving her Pretoria home, her animals and her lifelong friends was a real wrench for her. The pull to move was that both of her children, and her nine grandchildren, would be in Sydney. And so she came, and over the next 13 years made a life for herself. Her grandchildren loved her dearly and made the most of the opportunity to spend time with her. She adored them, too. Her eyes would light up when one or more arrived to spend an afternoon or take her out to tea. She particularly loved it when my son Sean arrived with our Cavalier King Charles, Jamie, in tow. Sean inherited my mother's love for animals, and he and she and the affectionate dog spent many hours together.

Mum's final 18 months were, however, very tough ones for all of us. After several falls, hospitalisations and operations, the decision was made for her to enter a nursing home. With her fiercely independent spirit, she hated its confines. It was nothing to do with the home itself or with the staff, who were caring and kind; in retrospect, it just wasn't the place for her. A regret for me in life is that I did not do something about this, nor did I personally give her the amount of time that she desperately wanted and deserved. Quality time and quantity of time – both were needed, and I know I didn't do enough.

In the latter months of 2010, Mum's physical and mental condition rapidly deteriorated. She wanted to die and she told us so. Over this period, she ate very little and became frail. Still, her eyes lit up when any of the family arrived, and I know she felt special joy when it was me, her only daughter. Her nursing home was a long way from my office in the city and from my home in Terrey Hills. In those last few weeks, I went as often as I could – three or four times during the week and on the weekend. In the final few days, I was with her constantly. It was a special time, with family arriving and stories and memories being recounted. Mum eventually fell into a coma. The nursing home moved a bed into her room for me and I lay down beside my mother, holding her hand. She died on 10 December in the early hours of the morning. It means a lot to me that I was there, holding her hand and telling her that I loved her.

The bank's annual general meeting was scheduled for 15 December. I knew that I could make arrangements for the funeral in such a way that I could be there for this important share-holder meeting, but I decided that I was not going to do that. I decided I was going to dedicate this period to properly honouring my mother, to give her all my time and attention, be with family and reflect on her life and our lives together. Not surprisingly, Ted Evans, Westpac's chairman, was strongly supportive. I asked Phil Coffey, our chief financial officer, to act in my stead and deliver the CEO address I had written in the days preceding my mother's death. I knew I was making the right decision, but I was also aware that this decision was different from the one I would have made five years earlier in the same circumstances. I would have rushed around trying to do it all. I would have been at the AGM and I would have been at the funeral. But I would have missed some-thing precious, something that I could never recover or regain.

Today when people ask me what I am most proud of in my life and career to date, the answer is an easy one: I am proud of my family. My 40-year happy marriage with Allan, and our four won-derful, centred and caring children: Sharon, a schoolteacher; Sean, a medical doctor; Mark, a mechanical engineer; and Annie, a mar-keting executive. While luck has a lot to do with this, so has our focus on family – putting family first.

2

BEING IN
THE MOMENT

'Being in the moment' is something I have really had to work on over the years. As my family would attest, I tend to do everything at pace and several things simultaneously. On my 50th birthday, Sharon presented me with *Little Miss Somersault* by Roger Hargreaves (one of the 'Mr Men' and 'Little Miss' series) and gave a speech about me with the book as its theme. Apparently, Little Miss Somersault is full of energy. Rather than walking, she cartwheels. Instead of going through the front door, she will climb on the roof and she won't need a ladder. So stopping, pausing and ensuring that I am truly in the moment for the person I am with, or the situation I am in, has taken conscious effort.

Many family stories would reveal what a slow learner I have been. Here are two, both involving my son Mark. The first story has a funny side; the second is rather more poignant.

In the mid-1990s, when the triplets were around six years old, I decided that, on an individual and rotational basis, I would take each one to school. From the outset, Allan and I had resolved to send Sean, Mark and Annie to separate schools. We wanted to encourage their individual development, let each one grow at his or her own pace, without comparison. It was Week 1 of this new plan, and it was Mark's turn. I settled him into the back seat of the car and off we went. Down the driveway we headed, turning right into Kilkenny Road when the car phone rang. It was one of my colleagues providing feedback on negotiations underway on a business transaction. The conversation moved to other topics and, as we concluded the call, I drove into my designated parking bay at my city office. A little voice piped up behind me: 'Mum, have you forgotten me? Aren't we going to school?' Oh dear. My sweet son. So much for the new resolution of one-on-one quality time.

The second story is from later in the same year. The occasion was Mark's school concert. He and all the other boys and girls in Year 1 were representing a letter of the alphabet. Mark was assigned the letter E and was going to be Ellie the Elephant. In the days before the concert, Mark, Allan and I constructed a rather large and unwieldy papier-mâché trunk and elephant ears. For the big occasion, when it came to E, our little boy would step out of the line and walk up and down the stage flapping his ears, swinging his trunk and making trumpeting sounds. I arrived a little ahead of time on the evening of the concert and carefully chose a seat on the aisle, about three-quarters of the way back. I had a good look at the program to see when the first-graders would be on, and then stepped outside to make some business calls. I became absorbed. As I finished, I looked at my watch. A moment of panic – I hope I haven't misjudged this. I rushed back in and found my seat. Golly the Gorilla, with his big woolly head and black coat of hair, was up and about on the stage – I had missed it. How embarrassed and ashamed I felt. A knot of pain settled in the pit of my stomach. It was many years before I was able to confess this story to my son, who gave me the biggest smile and told me not to worry so much.

There are a lot of reasons why 'being in the moment' is a powerful skill. It has forced me to slow down, to properly listen and focus. There is no doubt that I feel happier in myself when I am giving all I can to the person or situation in front of me. In that way, being in the moment is fulfilling and liberating. It has also meant that I prioritise very carefully and explicitly make trade-off decisions. I know in advance that if I commit to a meeting or engagement, I am going to give it my complete undivided attention. I will be there physically, mentally, emotionally. Of course, being in the moment is not just for scheduled activities – it is an everyday way of living your life that requires strong levels of self-awareness and discipline. As I walk into the foyer of our office building, as I enter an elevator or stand at a checkout, I strive to be in the moment. I make sure I see, actually see, people around me, look them in the eye, smile, thank, connect – small things that matter, small ways to help everyone, including myself, have a better day.

The rewards of this life lesson are probably most amplified at home. It can be hardest to achieve at home, particularly in today's world of being constantly 'on' with smartphones and social media. A family around the dinner table are all physically there but may not be really present as each engages with his or her device, each in a separate world. My family know I hate this, so mobile phones can only be used at mealtimes if they serve to support the conversation at hand. I do my bit, too – I work hard to schedule evening, weekend and holiday work calls and commitments at times that don't conflict with family time.

Let me conclude this chapter with some thoughts on the issue of 'quality versus quantity time'. A few years ago I shared a stage with a fellow CEO of an Australian ASX200 company. In question time, a young woman asked us for tips on achieving balance between work and family life. My colleague indicated that for him, it was about quality time with his children. While it may only be a few hours a week, he ensured the time spent together was of genuinely high quality. He provided examples. I found I needed to add something to the conversation. What I have learned over my life and my career is that quality of time and quantity of time are both very important. In my experience, it matters to be part of the cut and thrust of everyday life – being home whenever possible for dinners, for family chores, for simply lounging about with the kids, being part of the routine matters that make up lives.

For my 54th birthday, Sharon gave me a book entitled *Mum*. It is made up of various sections, such as 'Earliest memories of you', 'Do you remember when' and 'Favourites from Mum's kitchen' with space for the daughter or son to write in. In the section entitled 'Something you probably don't know' Sharon had written:

'I really liked it when you came to kiss us each morning. You may have thought I was sleeping, but I always knew you were there.'

I didn't know it at the time, but those were small 'in the moment' moments that counted.

3

A WOMAN
IN BUSINESS

Throughout my career, I have found this to be one of the most difficult topics to talk about, and I find it no easier to write about. In as straightforward a way as possible, I will seek to tell my story. Not for a moment am I suggesting that it provides lessons for anyone else – each woman has her own unique set of circumstances, her own dreams, her own challenges, and her own choices to make. If, however, my story sparks thoughts or ideas that are helpful to women, or assists leaders in thinking through how to provide support and opportunities for women, I will be delighted.

Here is my story, which in the interests of clarity I shall structure as follows:

- What has helped me
- What I have found difficult

—————— WHAT HAS HELPED ME ——————

1. Strong support throughout my career.

This support came in a number of ways. To start with, I appreciate that I was very lucky to work in organisations that embraced me and provided opportunities. I think specifically of the Perm in my early years, which, among other things, encouraged me to do an MBA and supported me financially over the duration. I reflect on Nedcor Bank for not only being prepared to employ me as General Manager, Human Resources, knowing full well that I had four children aged four and under, but also for its willingness to trust and empower me to make it work. I reflect on the Commonwealth Bank going far beyond what one could reasonably expect in supporting the family in our migration to Australia before, during and in the crucial years immediately after our move.

I think back too on line managers I have had over my career who sponsored me and encouraged me. Mike Leeming, executive director, Nedcor Bank, provided the very best in coaching and support in the years 1992 to 1997 – my early years of being a business leader. Mike has continued as a mentor and friend throughout my career. John Mulcahy welcomed me onto his new team at the Commonwealth Bank without being involved in the interview process at all, and helped me find my feet in Australian banking.

David Murray made a left-field and bold decision, unforeseen by most, to appoint me to his executive team and run the 20 000-person branch and business-banking distribution business called Customer Service Division. Frank Conroy, chairman of St.George, selected me to be the CEO of St.George ahead of candidates who were better known and more seasoned in banking. For the next several years, Frank's strong leadership and chairmanship skills helped me make the transition to being a CEO. At Westpac, my two very different chairmen and my deputy chairman each gave me exactly the support and direction I needed as I developed through the different phases of my CEO years. Ted Evans, with his calm demeanour and wise, considered approach; Lindsay Maxsted, smart, analytical, commercial; and John Curtis, demanding and encouraging in equal measure.

Next, colleagues and friends. Throughout my career, I have had people around me whom I knew I could 100 per cent rely on – team members, former colleagues, external advisers, board members, people who seemed always available to help, challenge and support. Crucially, these individuals would tell me what they thought I needed to hear. They knew I would listen, and even if I disagreed with their counsel, I was likely to moderate something in how I proceeded. No recognition or public thanks was ever sought. Today, most are firm friends.

My Westpac farewell event in February 2015 was a private affair made up of these very people. Lindsay Maxsted hosted the evening, Peter Hanlon served as master of ceremonies and John Arthur gave the main speech. My connection with John dates back to my very first day at the Commonwealth Bank, 27 October 1997 – seven days after my arrival in Australia. Over close to 20 years, he has advised me, encouraged me, backed me and kept me out of trouble. It is impossible to put a value on this kind of loyalty, this kind of friendship.

2. A marriage that is a partnership

I am on record as saying that without my husband, Allan, my career in business would not have been possible. I cannot overstate this. Allan and I married in Pretoria, South Africa in our very young twenties, without much thought about practicalities or long-term plans. The first year of our married life was spent in Rhodesia, a country engaged in a fierce and bitter civil war. Allan's year involved full-time compulsory national service duty; I was based at Falcon College, teaching Latin. It was certainly an unusual way to start out in marriage, with months at a time passing without our seeing each other.

Next stop was Johannesburg, where Allan commenced his medical degree at the University of the Witwatersrand. After a short, unhappy stint in teaching, I moved into banking and found that I loved it. The year 1985 turned out to be a particularly busy one for us, with Allan completing his internship and me underway with a full-time MBA. In 1986, our first daughter arrived and in 1989, the triplets. My career took off in 1990 with my appointment to General Manager, Human Resources. Under the circumstances, with very young children, I agonised over whether to take the role and it was Allan who encouraged me. Similarly, it was he who gave me the push in 1992 to accept the position of general manager of the card business.

Those early years set the pattern of how we made it work. Ours was and is a partnership. We shared out what needed to get done.

Allan has never had a problem doing the washing, ironing, clean-ing, fetching and carrying – whatever is required. His preparedness to take on roles more usually done by the wife and mother was something I particularly appreciated once we were in Australia, when for years we operated without much household assistance. Life was pretty exhausting. Everyone needed to step up and help. We were happy to accept that things would not be perfect.

Our most important priority was our children. We worked on spending lots of time together as a family, with evening din-ners, weekend activities and holidays. By conscious choice, Allan's job had more predictable hours than mine, and on a day-to-day basis that gave us a framework within which to operate. I was never someone to linger unnecessarily at work, and the family knew I would be home as soon as I could. Things didn't always work out as planned, of course, and sometimes I would be held up or called away. I received unquestioning loyalty and support from Allan, who trusted me to make it work as best I could. When I was dis-couraged or stressed, he helped by being so clearly 'on my side'. My beautiful children have always been the same. They have had to put up with a greater degree of chaos around them than most, yet each has been unwavering in his or her care for me and provided, together with their father, a bedrock of support.

The philosopher Kahlil Gibran in his best-known work, *The Prophet*, muses on a wide number of life topics, including mar-riage. He speaks of letting there be 'spaces in your togetherness' and of giving your hearts 'but not into each other's keeping'. He comments that 'the pillars of the temple stand apart' and that 'the oak tree and the cypress grow not in each other's shadow'. Going all the way back to our University of Cape Town days, Allan and I liked this philosophy. And it has worked for us, made possible by the combination of Allan's unselfishness, my positive attitude, and a focus, through the good times and the rough patches, on strong communication.

3. Hard work and getting things done

If you read through the school reports that my mum kept so carefully for me (even bringing them with her to Australia), the theme emerges of a conscientious and hardworking young girl. I seem to have taken my school life very seriously. Clearly, working hard is in my DNA. The point of the tennis wall my father built at my childhood home in Pretoria was to encourage hours of practice; similarly, the cricket nets for my brother. My father would have been an advocate for Malcolm Gladwell's '10 000 Hour Rule' – the 10 000 hours of practice required to achieve mastery, whatever the field of endeavour. For my father, working hard was a fundamental and necessary requirement for achievement at the highest level. It wasn't the only requirement – natural talent and aptitude were critical, and luck played its part – but nothing could replace disciplined hard work.

I absorbed these lessons early and, over my career, was always willing to put in the effort and shoulder the load. I learned how to work quickly and effectively, and brought energy and enthusiasm to the task. This meant that I was noticed and that further opportunities came my way. Sometimes I am asked: 'Do you think you had to work harder in your career because you are a woman?' The answer is 'I don't know, but I don't think so'. From what I could see, the senior men around me worked just as hard. It is probably true, however, that it took longer for me to prove myself relative to equally performing male colleagues, particularly in my most senior leadership roles. My response was to keep at it, focusing on delivery and playing the long game.

4. Being prepared to put my hand up

As discussed in the chapter 'Be Bold, Dig Deep, Back Yourself', it took courage for me to put my hand up and have a go. In retrospect, I was far too frightened of failure. Yet, when confronting big 'fork-in-the-road' decisions, I found it in myself to dig deep and say yes.

My first appointment to the position of CEO illustrates this well. On 16 September 2001, Ed O'Neal, the CEO of St.George, died suddenly at his Sydney home. I recall hearing the sad news and reflecting on how difficult it must be for his wife and son, who were not with him at the time of his heart attack. It did not enter my mind that the announcement had any relevance for my career. I was the Group Executive, Customer Service Division for the Commonwealth Bank and loving my job. The acquisition of Colonial had recently occurred and I had my hands full with merger and integration activities. So it was a surprise for me to receive a call from Robert Webster of Korn Ferry, an executive search firm, asking whether I might be interested in being considered for the position.

At the time the call came through I was in Singapore with my family; I indicated I would reflect on the matter and let him know. Saying yes to being part of the process did not require that much courage because from my perspective I had no prospect of actually landing the job. I decided it would be good for me to go through the assessment and interview experience as I would learn something.

Approaching the process in this way meant that I was more relaxed at the interview than I would otherwise have been. The full board was present, and I recall a question from John Curtis, a senior director of the bank and later its chairman. He asked me what I would do in the first six months to drive shareholder value and mount a defence if a major bank came knocking. (At that point, National Australia Bank had an ownership stake in the bank close to the maximum allowable, and was viewed as a very likely acquirer.) While the question has stuck in my memory, I don't recall my answer. I must have done okay, because very shortly thereafter, Frank Conroy, the bank's chairman, scheduled a one-on-one conversation with me at his Sydney apartment and offered me the role. Frank was keen to have an answer quickly. This was Thursday; I promised to call on Monday morning.

It was a stressful weekend. I set out the pros and cons, with the biggest cons relating to the fact that I was very happy where I was and that the future of St.George as a standalone entity was decidedly uncertain. What I didn't state, that only Allan would know, was a deep fear of 'Can I do this job? Do I have what it takes?' and the dreaded 'What if I fail?' Now was the time to be courageous and just say yes. I am very glad I did.

5. Getting on with people

I like people and am interested in people. I like the fact that people are different, with individual styles and approaches, idiosyncrasies, personal circumstances, ways of looking at the world. I have always been perceptive, noticing the small things that tell you how people are feeling – body language, facial expression, general demeanour. I am able to read silences, pick up on non-verbal cues and detect shifts in mood or behaviour. I am also reasonably self-aware about my own behaviour and how others are seeing me, and am able to adapt if required. I love to be part of a winning team, and look for opportunities to help others. At the same time I am careful not to take credit publicly or privately for the achievements of colleagues. I dislike political behaviour in organisations and I avoid environments where undermining of others occurs. I look for things to celebrate, to acknowledge. I am optimistic and constructive by nature, willing to listen, and prepared to change my mind. I tend to say yes far more than I say no. I love to see others succeed, and I work hard not to let others down. I am consistent, day in, day out.

All of these elements combine to assist in getting on with people. This meant that, as my career progressed, I was backed, supported, helped and encouraged. In the important early years, I was readily included in discussions and meetings, assigned to strategic projects, given access to critical and sensitive information and trusted with it. My opinion was sought and respected. When I dug myself into a hole, colleagues came to my aid and helped me find a way out. Later in my career, getting on with others helped me build great teams and receive support as the leader. I became better at applying the 'right person, right role' principle, and more generous-spirited in my approach to the job.

This is not to say that I haven't had my share of difficult people issues along the way. There are those who have undermined me, diminished me, ignored me, been threatened by me, and gone into battle against me. Being 'good with people' helps in these situations, too – very rarely was I caught unawares, due to both my own instinctive sense of the situation and the warnings of friends and colleagues.

It is self-evident, I think, that if you want to get on in business, you need to be able to get on with people. This is all the more the case for a businesswoman in a traditionally male world. She will face additional barriers, some clear to see and others more subtle. If she can get on with people – colleagues, bosses, board members, customers, employees at the coalface – then her job will be a lot easier and she will be a lot happier.

6. The power of a great team

Going back to my South African days at Nedcor Bank, my boss, Mike Leeming, would say, 'The secret to Gail Kelly's leadership was building a great team around her and letting them get on with the job'. There is a lot of truth to this. I understood early that I needed the very best people on my side – people who were better than me. I understood the truth in the statement, 'The whole is greater than the sum of its parts', that the combination of top-class individuals in a strongly aligned and synergistic team is very powerful. Throughout my career, this is the model I have striven for.

Building and managing a great team demands considerable focus from the leader. I have invested heavily in this. Firstly, I established a personal relationship with each individual on the team. The fuller the appreciation I had of his or her dreams, ambitions, concerns, hot buttons, vulnerabilities and personal circumstances, the better the support I would be able to provide. Secondly, I encouraged team members to spend time together, getting to know each other and developing an understanding of how best to combine and align. Thirdly, I ensured that we had plenty of time as a team on current issues, on long-term strategy, and on how we were performing. We developed a charter in respect of behaviours to which we subscribed, and regularly assessed our progress.

For me, it was no surprise that the periods of my career when I was most successful were the periods when I had a great team around me. These were extraordinarily rewarding times, personally and professionally. Each of my key leadership roles included a sustained period when this was the situation, and it made all the difference.

7. Being myself

Very early in my career, at the time of my first role leading people, I was drawn aside by a senior executive and given some advice. He told me that I needed to change some things. Now that I was going to be the boss of the team, it was important to create some distance between myself and those reporting to me. I needed to keep them guessing, to let them know by my behaviour that I was in charge.

The advice made me anxious and I did not follow it. I knew intuitively that it was not the approach that would work for me, and that to be successful, I needed to remain true to myself.

As I became more senior, the fact that I was a woman occupying an executive role in an industry dominated by men drew more comment. Again, I knew that the key to my success was to remain consistent and be myself. My style has always been a personal and natural one. In terms of clothes, I love colour and have suits and dresses of all shades in my wardrobe. In fact on 'results days', our finance team would run an internal competition to guess what colour I would be wearing! It generated a lot of fun on what was otherwise a pretty serious day. My CFO, Phil Coffey, had several ties on hand to make sure our colours did not clash.

When it comes to writing or speaking, my messages have

always been my own. I usually deliver speeches without using notes. Regardless of the audience, I am consistent in what I have to say. Throughout my career I have loved to engage with customers, shareholders and employees. People approach me in all sorts of locations – shopping centres, airport terminals, city streets, the beach – to introduce themselves and have a chat. When visiting teams across the business, I travelled without 'minders' – I like the freedom to do things on the spur of the moment, such as pop into a branch on the way home, or visit one of our head-office floors. This has been my consistent pattern.

One of the roles I most value and enjoy is my membership of the Group of Thirty (G30). This private, non-profit organisation is a consultative body on international economic and monetary affairs. Its members are extraordinarily interesting and accomplished people – central bankers and previous central bankers, academics, economists and practitioners. I was asked to deliver a presentation to the group at their 2013 Spring Plenary in Shanghai and was then extended an invitation to become one of their members. It was hard not to feel a little intimidated at first. My skill set is different from that of my colleagues, most of whom come from a policy or an academic background. There was no point in trying to match them in their domains: to be an effective contributor, I knew that I needed to be myself and bring my 'feet on the ground' practitioner's perspective, outlining the implications and effects of policy and discussing the forces of change in the industry. I bring diversity to the G30 not only because I am a woman, but because my experience base and my perspectives are different. Remaining true to myself is what my fellow members want from me, and it is the only thing I can do.

8. Good bandwidth coupled with perspective

In my experience, women tend to have excellent bandwidth – we tackle a lot of different things simultaneously and can absorb extraordinary pressures and stresses because we have to. This is an advantage we bring to the workplace. We are multidimensional and can scale up and scale down as required. It is really helpful if this ability to deal with conflicting pressures and priorities is accompanied with perspective about what's important. I think I have developed this over time, probably from sheer necessity. I don't often get flustered and have an instinctive sense of what's really critical, what I personally need to worry about.

While this is clearly a very useful skill and saves everyone a lot of stress, my application of it was sometimes annoying for others, particularly those closest to me. On many an occasion I would come home to a minor catastrophe and brush it off as unimportant in the overall scheme of things. I remember returning to our Parkview home in Johannesburg one evening to find Allan waiting for me. He greeted me as I walked in the door and directed me to our beautiful, freshly painted white wall that our five-year-olds had covered in crayon. 'It's only a wall,' I said. While this was true, it was not the response Allan was looking for.

9. Just getting on with things

All women in business have at some time or other had to deal with being ignored, overlooked or taken for granted – for example, arriving at a dinner event where you are passed over while your male partner is warmly welcomed and greeted; or having a personal assistant at the end of the telephone ask whose PA you are when you seek to be connected to your general manager colleague.

I chose to take these sorts of instances in my stride as well as the inevitable comments in the media about what I was wearing or about some element of my physical features. The 'Banking Uber Babe', as I was once described, was certainly not how I thought of myself!

More difficult to ignore were the subtle and sometimes not-so-subtle sexual innuendos that were seemingly common-place, particularly in the workplace of the 1990s and early 2000s. Fortunately for me, none were serious enough to warrant escalation, and generally I was able to put the individual in his place.

My scariest moment occurred when I was on Nedcor Bank duty in Vienna in the mid-1990s. I was there to present on the business applications of smart-card technology at a Visa conference. My mother and my daughter Sharon had accompanied me on the trip. On the morning of my presentation, as I walked through the park near the conference centre rehearsing my speech, I was jumped from behind and forcefully pushed to the ground. I screamed so loudly and kicked so fiercely that the man took fright and ran off. Fortunately a passer-by came to my aid, and further assisted me in reporting the incident to police; the perpetrator was subsequently apprehended. I carried on to do my presentation, but for the rest of our time in Vienna, my mother, daughter and I were assigned a Visa security officer to escort us everywhere.

I learned from this and other unpleasant experiences that I needed to take extra care and be ever-vigilant when travelling overseas. I seemed at the time to just accept that such was the world we were living in. It is, of course, completely unacceptable, and today I am much less accommodating. Women in business – women in any walk of life – should not have to put up with this.

10. A sense of humour

On a lighter note, I have also found that having a sense of humour is invaluable. Lots of little things happen in a career to which you can either choose to take offence, or smile. For me, smiling was usually the better option.

I recall a Qantas plane trip from Melbourne to Sydney, late in my Westpac career. There was no-one sitting next to me and the flight attendant approached me with a question, which he put to me very earnestly.

'Mrs Kelly, do you mind if I ask you – do you enjoy your job as CEO of Westpac?'

'Yes, very much so.'

Surprised, he asked me a second question, no doubt the underlying question: 'So, do you find that it is something you can manage?'

'Yes,' I assured him again.

'Really?' He looked somewhat disbelieving. 'But how do you do it? Being the CEO of a bank is really a job for a man, isn't it?'

There was nothing for it but to smile.

My smile was even broader when I was at St.George and discovered my young daughter didn't quite know what I did. One Friday evening, Allan drove into the city with the children to meet me after work and parked in the St.George building at Circular Quay in the spot designated 'Managing Director, St.George Bank'.

'You can't park here, Dad,' said Annie.

'Why not?' said Allan.

'Well, this space is reserved for the managing director.'

'That's what Mum is.'

'Of the whole bank? No, she's not,' said my daughter, incredulous that her mum, who struggled to change a light bulb at home, could possibly have this role.

11. Being different

For almost all of my career, my counterparts in similar roles have been men. I have therefore stood out as different and a focus of attention. This can be both helpful and, as I discuss in the next section, present difficulties. The helpful element lies first in being noticed, and secondly in being provided opportunities as organisations seek to achieve a better gender mix. Like all women in business I know, being appointed on merit for a position really matters. Having said that, in the case of an organisation keen to introduce more diversity into its management ranks, being a competent woman is advantageous. For example, although I have no doubt that I merited my appointment to General Manager, Strategic Marketing in the Commonwealth Bank, I think it likely that my gender helped. Australia in 1997 had very few female general managers in banking, and several organisations were keen to address the gap. Arising from my one-week round of interviews in Sydney and Melbourne in June 1997, I received general management job offers from five different financial-services organisations. I doubt whether a similarly qualified man from South Africa would have been as warmly received.

Being different also clearly defined me in my role as CEO of St.George. I turned out to be a very good fit for the brand, bringing warmth, connectedness and a human touch to the way the business was run. This was different from the typical style of banking CEOs and was noticed by customers, employees and media, all of whom treated me very well. Interestingly, in terms of competitors

I was largely underestimated. I was able to keep my head down and operate under the radar. This helped St.George in its position of being an alternative to the major banks: big enough to meet all your needs, yet small enough to remain personal, connected and friendly. In this case, being different was good for me in a personal capacity, as well as being good for our brand and our business strategy.

WHAT I HAVE FOUND DIFFICULT

1. Being different

The heightened level of visibility and of scrutiny that comes with being a senior woman in business was something I accepted as coming with the job. To mitigate it, particularly in the second half of my Westpac career, I avoided profile pieces in newspapers and magazines; I was extremely selective regarding when I would appear on television – there had to be a compelling reason for me to do it; and I chose private rather than public platforms for my major speeches. This worked for me.

What I found more challenging was dealing with senior people in the industry, mostly men, who had a preconceived view of the necessary ingredients for an effective major bank CEO. Unconsciously or consciously, their view was based on what they were familiar with: a male CEO. Because I did not pass that first test, I found I had to work harder to 'prove myself'.

This was compounded, I think, by the fact that not only was my gender different from what people were used to, but my way of leading was different too. Mine was not a top-down authoritative style of leadership, and nor did I use the language of banking to anything like the degree that my male counterparts, coming from the institutional or finance arms of the business, tended to do. I would bristle with annoyance when I read comments from analysts or fund managers along the lines of 'Granted she is good with the "soft" stuff of people and culture, but it's just as well she has strong bankers around her to handle the financial aspects.' Once Andrew Bowden, Westpac's longstanding and excellent head of investor relations, had calmed me down, we would discuss what I needed to do to deal with that perception.

In truth, I believe that it was not fully understood how my more inclusive style of leadership – right person, right role; team-based; each individual both fully empowered yet fully accountable – worked in practice. By the end of my time at Westpac, two things had happened: I had successfully adjusted my language and approach for this audience, and Westpac was gaining recognition for high-quality results over a sustained period. I finally achieved a pass mark, and hopefully succeeded in shifting the preconceived view. The emails and notes I received from members of the analyst and investor community at the time of my retirement were particularly gratifying.

2. Dealing to expectations

The expectations I refer to here are the expectations from other businesswomen for me to be a spokesperson in the sometimes-fraught area of gender equality and women's choices. Being appointed the CEO of St.George was the trigger for these expectations to develop. Rather than publicly address them, I preferred to ensure that I delivered in the job, and then to let my performance and my role-modelling speak for themselves.

Once I was appointed CEO of Westpac, the expectations and, indeed, requirements of me grew considerably. I was slow to deal with this. As discussed in the chapter 'Diversity is Strength', I found myself consumed with issues of the global financial crisis and the planned merger with St.George. Within Westpac itself, I incorrectly judged that the excellent momentum happening in relation to women in management would sustain itself. Therefore, neither publicly nor within Westpac did I properly prioritise advocacy. By late 2009, I realised the mistake I had made and moved fast to adjust it. I am very proud of the strategy we implemented and how we set about embedding a culture of diversity, building it into the fabric of the organisation. I am particularly proud of the significant and growing numbers of strong, capable women at Westpac who are integral to its success. In terms of the public arena, I looked for and embraced opportunities to address the issues of women in business, using platforms such as International Women's Day, Westpac's *The Power of 100* book launch, the Westpac/*Australian Financial Review* '100 Women of Influence' awards, and my role as CARE Australia's ambassador for women's empowerment.

My overall assessment is that I made this issue more difficult for myself than I needed to. I remain of the view that above all else it was critical to deliver in the role itself. The truth is, however, that I had the platform to do more and I should not have needed to be nudged.

3. Achieving balance

Often the very first question I get asked when speaking on diversity issues is 'How did you do what you did and still achieve balance in your life?' There is no short answer to this, no formula. Life is a messy business, and we each need to plot our own course and make our own mistakes along the way. I know I made plenty of them, and over the years I have struggled with feelings of guilt and regret that I was not there, that I was not able to attend something important in the life of one of the children. I then made it worse for myself by not letting go of the emotion. The time is past, the choice was made, the event was missed, the child is fine – why can I not move on? I still get a lump in my throat when I reflect on some of the life events I was not around for: my son Mark in his first year of school falling off a jungle gym, badly winded, small ribcage painful to touch, upset and asking for his mother, who is hours away from home at a conference; my daughter Annie who said, 'Don't worry, Mum, it's all right – there will be another one' when I let her down at the last minute by not being able to go to the mother–daughter school tea she had been excited about; my son Sean trying to hide his disappointment that his mother was not there to see him receive the 'First in Class' Year 5 award at the Sydney Grammar Preparatory School prize-giving. There are lots of these stories, small in themselves but important. It is interesting that I don't have any feelings of regret or guilt about those business engagements I missed when prioritising family events above them.

I think I got better at achieving balance as my career progressed. It was no doubt also a little easier as the children passed the primary-school stage. From the time I was at St.George, I began to prioritise all elements of my life in an integrated way. The 'big rocks' of birthdays, anniversaries, holidays and major school events were put into my calendar at the outset. For each child, I would schedule the activities that mattered most to him or her. Allan and I shared out events such as parent–teacher days and school concerts. Important work commitments, such as board meetings, annual general meetings and financial results days were, of course, also noted. I found it very useful to develop the calendar for the full year, then have a detailed look at the following three months. I would check to see that I was prioritising important things, not just urgent things. I made sure I was in control of the schedule, rather than it controlling me. I would ensure an appropriate amount of 'white space' time for thinking, preparation, regeneration, and for dealing with emergency issues. I also became more skilled at being 'in the moment' – in other words, whatever I was doing, committing fully to that situation, person or group of people, being 100 per cent present. I think this is a critical skill, and one that can be learned. It can be harder to apply at home, and yet that's where it really matters.

On occasion, I have found myself being presented as an example that women can 'have it all'. This is not something I have welcomed, nor is the idea something I endorse. What 'all' means will differ from person to person, and can also change at different times of your life. Each of us makes choices, and these choices have consequences. In choosing to work as I did, personal relationships outside the home, particularly with my women friends, were neglected. The long hours, persistent pressure and travel requirements also meant that I was not able to be around for my children, for their young years and their everyday activities, nearly as much as I would have liked. It is very important to add, however, that I never saw being a businesswoman and being a mother as requiring a trade-off decision. I always wanted both. Today I strongly encourage young women who also want both to go for it. In my experience, you will work it out from there. One of the really important things I have learned is not to beat myself up too much. This is a learning I highly recommend to others.

———————

In this chapter I have told my story of being a woman in business. I know it has another instalment yet to come – an instalment where I will have more freedom, more capacity and more experience to play a role in the push for gender equality. I have a particular passion for engaging with young people at schools and universities and seeking to help them as they dream and plan their futures. I also have a passion for supporting work in developing nations and disadvantaged communities, as the cultural, economic and structural barriers facing women in these environments are substantial. Ninety per cent of countries have at least one legal measure that restricts women's economic opportunities. Girls are more likely to miss school so they can assist with household chores, more likely to suffer neglect, and more at risk of violence and sexual abuse. There is a lot of work to be done, and I look forward to deepening my engagement in these important areas.

4

MAKING A
DIFFERENCE

'The goal of a firm is to maximise shareholder value.' This was the core tenet of my 1985–86 MBA program, and it reflected the management thinking of the time. We were well acquainted with the 'business of business is business' doctrine, and with the free market orthodoxy that underpinned it. When it came to what, if any, was the social responsibility of a business, the well-known philosophy of the Nobel prize-winning economist Milton Friedman had primacy. In a nutshell: focus your activities on increasing your profits – this is your sole purpose; an open and efficient market will do the rest.[47]

As a young executive, I found myself uncomfortable with this rather narrow view. Business-school conversations centred on what I saw as a flawed trade-off – between the interests of shareholders on one hand and the interests of customers, employees and the community on the other. Was it not possible to run a business for the long-term interests of all? Indeed, was it not possible that the interests of shareholders were best served by a company consistently doing the right thing within society? I recall voicing these questions and making the case for a broader view of the role of business, at an international mortgage conference held in May 1986 at the University of Cambridge in England. 'Banking is not about profit maximisation,' I volunteered. I was comprehensively shouted down. I must be very naive, I thought – a notion reinforced by the fact that I was the only woman among the 100-plus delegates at the conference.

By the early 2000s, the concept of Corporate Social Responsibility (CSR) was in vogue. Much of the activity, however, fell into the category of being 'add-ons' to the core business. Corporate donations and sponsorships of worthy causes grew. By 2009–10, the call was for something much more meaningful – a fundamental reassessment of the role of business in society together with an overhaul of how companies were actually run. It was now clear that an obsessive and singular focus on maximising shareholder returns all too frequently resulted in one or more of the following: short-term orientation, self-interest, financial

---

47   In his famous September 1970 essay written for the *New York Times Magazine*, Milton Friedman had hard-hitting words for people who spoke of the need for a social conscience in business. Not only did he see this as a nonsense, but he saw it as a dangerous nonsense, one that undermined and harmed the foundation for a free society.

engineering, tax-minimisation strategies, ruthlessness towards suppliers, disdain towards customers, and cost-cutting without sufficient focus on investment for the future. In certain cases, it also led to gaming the system and to fraud. Witness the accounting scandals of 2001–02, with Enron, WorldCom and Tyco being prime examples. Witness, too, the failures of the 2008–09 banking crisis. It is not difficult to find shocking empirical evidence of corporate greed and malfeasance. Economies were derailed, societies harmed and people badly hurt. Particularly in the US, Europe and the UK, numerous banks and bankers found themselves in the spotlight. The anger and distrust directed towards them continues to be severe. Australian banks have not been exempt from this – indeed, in the wake of a number of scandals and ethical breaches, the trust gap between the community and the industry has grown. Calls for a royal commission into banking have been the result. Individually and collectively, bankers are responding and taking on the challenge of cultural change in order to better fulfil their social contract.

The reality is that soundly managed commercial banks are particularly well placed to make a positive difference in society. Banking activities are inextricably linked with the economic and social fabric of the communities in which they operate. Banks provide direct employment to people from the community and offer training, development and career opportunities. They support their business customers, large and small, providing funding, advice, payment and risk-management services; similarly, with regard to retail customers, banks offer the full range of services facilitating the business of day-to-day living as well as the fulfilment of dreams. Well-run commercial banks pay their taxes and provide a steady and consistent dividend stream to their shareholders. They connect with the community in supporting local charities, stepping up when disaster strikes, and partnering with government and local authorities on development projects. They provide 'thought leadership' on key issues of the day – for example, on climate-change initiatives, flexible workplace practices and economic policy. I have always felt that it is a privilege to be a banker: you have the opportunity and the responsibility to drive a sustainable business for the benefit of all your stakeholders; you have the opportunity and responsibility to make a real difference.

On my retirement from Westpac in February 2015, I was frequently asked what I was most proud of – my most memorable times, any specific highlights? In terms of highlights, a standout for me was the launch on 2 April 2014 of the Westpac Bicentennial Foundation. To recognise the bank's 200-year history and to reflect its ongoing commitment to Australia's continued prosperity, we decided to give $100 million in the form of a charitable foundation.[48] Its purpose: education. Its recipients: 100 leaders and scholars each year, forever, in a wide array of disciplines – people with ideas and passion to help shape the future. It was an immense privilege to stand alongside the bank's chairman, Lindsay Maxsted, and launch the program. The strength and warmth of the response from all stakeholders, including competitors, took us by surprise. It was a remarkable day.

Without doubt, however, when I reflect on my Westpac career, my greatest source of pride came from the employees of our 200-year-old organisation. Westpac team members have a keen understanding of what it means to be part of a company whose

---

48 The bank's 200-year anniversary was 8 April 2017. We launched the Bicentennial Foundation three years earlier in order to have 200 scholars in place for the bicentennial year.

own history has tracked the history of modern Australia. They are passionate about the customers and communities they serve. With few exceptions, they set out to do the right thing and to live the bank's central purpose of helping.

This is not a new phenomenon for Westpac employees. Determination to make a difference is embedded in the fabric of the company. It can be seen in Westpac's longstanding engagement with Indigenous communities, and in its commitment to a sustainable environment, with the bank being one of the ten founding signatories to the Equator Principles.[49] Employees join the Westpac Group because of this focus on sustainability and on making a difference.

It matters to customers, too. On numerous occasions over the years I have had the experience of a customer stopping me in the street or in the supermarket to tell me the story of their connection with Westpac: how we supported them when no other bank would, how on a handshake with their local manager many years ago, the relationship began. 'Make sure you look after Our Bank' were often the parting words.

Of course, customers have also stopped me and told their stories of how we have let them down. I welcomed these conversations not only for the learnings themselves, but also because in approaching me, customers showed that they were not indifferent. They did not think it was a waste of time. They wanted the bank to get it right.

Over recent years, both Australia and New Zealand have experienced a number of very serious natural disasters. Bushfires, cyclones and floods unfortunately occur all too frequently in Australia,

---

49   The Equator Principles provides a framework for banks to assess and manage the social and environmental impact of large projects to which they may provide finance. The agreement was signed by David Morgan in 2003.

and earthquakes are a regular occurrence in New Zealand. These events have caused tragic loss of life and devastating damage. In each situation, I have had the privilege to observe how Westpac employees have stepped up quickly, taking on leadership roles for themselves and for the bank in frontline response. I deliberately use the word 'observe' rather than 'oversee' or 'direct'. Response from Westpac comes fast at the local level because team members are already active contributors in the community – they know what to do and are empowered to do it. There is no 'asking for permission' requirement.

A striking example of this was the Westpac response to the February 2009 Victorian bushfire tragedy,[50] in which 173 people lost their lives and over 400 more were injured. Thousands of homes were destroyed. Only a few hours after the worst of the fire had swept through, leaving disaster and heartbreak in its wake, the Westpac team in Victoria had mobilised. Peter Hanlon tells of receiving a call on the Sunday morning from his Victorian leader informing him that seven branches and 12 emergency sites were being opened to assist the devastated communities. Local authorities deemed Westpac to be an essential service – the only bank accorded this position. Our employees were able to reach the affected areas quickly and start providing help of all kinds: financial, practical and personal. In the bank's 2009 annual sustainability report, Peter described the events and commented: '[The] first phone call was the best call I've had in years . . . the call was not to seek my permission. I knew right then that we had really begun to make a difference.'

---

50 The event is known as 'Black Saturday'. Strong winds combined with extreme temperatures and very low humidity were the direct cause of Australia's worst ever bushfire tragedy.

One of my most humbling days as CEO of Westpac occurred in that same week when I travelled with Peter to one of the most affected areas, Kinglake. At the time access was restricted to emergency personnel. We arrived in the heart of the devastated community and I saw firsthand our bank in operation: a table, a cash box, a record-keeping book and our committed, caring employees serving the steady line of community members, stunned and shocked by what had happened to them, their families and their neighbours. Being the only bank on the ground, we acted for all banks, cashing the emergency cheques being issued at the neighbouring table, taking deposits and facilitating payments.

I then headed over to the newly set-up emergency distribution centre and worked alongside the Westpac volunteers who had accompanied Peter and me up the mountain to Kinglake in our volunteer bus. Our job was to help unload the trucks and lay out essential supplies. I was deeply affected by the acute pain being experienced in the community and at times I moved slowly, so much so that I was pulled up by the woman supervising activities: 'Looking around you is not going to get the truck unloaded. Come on, honey, there's work to do.' 'Yes, of course,' I said, and picked up my pace.

The strong link between people making a difference in their own individual capacities and the organisation making a difference is very clear in a story such as this. Across Westpac, people rallied to assist in deeply personal ways. Through our Matching Gifts program,[51] through volunteering, mobilising supplier support and

---

51   Matching Gifts is a program whereby the organisation matches, dollar for dollar, the contribution an employee makes to the charity of his or her choice. In respect of the Victorian bushfires, our employees contributed over $800 000, which the bank matched, establishing a total Matching Gifts amount in excess of $1.6 million. This was in addition to the $1 million contribution made by the bank in the first week.

assistance, through sending blankets and equipment of all kinds, Westpac team members were there. And again and again, in the situation of the destructive floods and cyclones in Queensland, the devastating earthquakes in Christchurch, and much more. Ordinary people doing extraordinary things, way beyond the call of duty.

One of the roles that I am privileged to hold is that of CARE Australia's ambassador for women's empowerment. What an outstanding organisation this is, again with ordinary, everyday people doing extraordinary work, making a difference to the lives of those less fortunate. CARE is an international humanitarian aid organisation fighting global poverty. It has a special focus on working with women and girls to bring about lasting change in their communities. As part of my role, I have travelled with CARE to Malawi, Cambodia and Vanuatu and have had the opportunity to experience how CARE Australia goes about its work and the difference it makes. CARE's model is to work with grassroots communities, tailor programs to meet specific needs and, through engagement with local authorities, ensure sustainability.

CARE's work on bilingual education in Cambodia provides an excellent example of how they operate. Team members on the ground identified the learning difficulties for children in remote ethnic communities in north-east Cambodia and discovered that at the heart of the challenge lay the fact that Khmer, Cambodia's national language, was the only language of instruction in schools. The children from these remote communities could neither speak nor understand it, so even if they could get to school, they were disadvantaged from the outset. What CARE did was particularly innovative. They designed an entire curriculum in local ethnic languages and set up bilingual schools. Khmer could then be phased in for the children, building their confidence as they learned. Critically, CARE engaged with the leaders of these remote provinces, who endorsed the program and institutionalised it. Teachers were selected by village elders and, with CARE's training and support, have become passionate role models for the children they teach. The success of the program has meant that the Cambodian government recently adopted a bilingual education policy for the country as a whole.

My daughter Annie and I had the opportunity to visit O'Yadao Lower Secondary School in a remote region of Cambodia. This boarding school, built and staffed with CARE's direct support, enables boys and girls from distant communities to attend school. While the sleeping, washing and kitchen facilities are extremely basic, what is inspiring is the excitement and energy of the children. We gathered in the largest classroom and engaged in a translated conversation. Hands shot up – mostly it was the girls' hands – and young person after young person told us her or his dream for the future.

'I would like to be a teacher, so that I can help others.'

'I would like to be a doctor.'

'I am planning to be a writer. I would like to travel the world.'

We asked them about the difficulties they encountered in their school lives. They paused to think before volunteering 'travel distance from home' as the major one. One girl told us she was there because her father was determined for her to go to school, even though the fathers of many other children in her village insisted that their daughters stay home to help. Another girl then asked me what my biggest difficulty had been when I was at school. Oh my goodness – I had no idea how to answer. I turned to Annie and suggested she have a go. 'Well,' she said, 'I am so grateful to be here and to share a small part of your lives. Thank you so much. I was lucky to go to a very good school.' She gathered her thoughts, then slowly continued: 'I have always struggled to believe in myself, and to have confidence that I can do what lies ahead. I have learned that it is really important to back yourself, and be prepared to try. It is really important to follow your dreams.' By then, she had tears in her eyes. I did, too.

On our return to Australia, Annie told me how profoundly she had been affected by the trip. She had seen the power of education to make a difference and had spent time with amazing, selfless people who were devoted to helping others. She realised that she had a lot more to learn and a lot more to give.

In this world of 'haves' and 'have-nots' an increasingly important and powerful way the 'haves' can make a difference is through philanthropy. The original Greek derivation of 'philanthropy' is 'love of humanity'. Although Australia lags behind certain nations, most notably the US, in the culture of giving through philanthropy it is heartening to see the momentum shift that is occurring. In the decade 1997 to 2007 a number of barriers to giving were removed and it became possible for families to create their own charitable foundations.[52] Because the funds in such a foundation can never be withdrawn, it is a foundation for all time. Because all the monies earned each year have to be distributed, families can get involved on a regular basis to decide which charities to support and why. In the Kelly family we have found this to be very powerful. The six of

---

52 Private Ancillary Funds (PAFs), essentially private charitable trusts, are outstanding vehicles for individuals, families and businesses to make tax-deductible gifts to organisations that have deductible gift recipient (DGR) status. The number of PAFs in Australia has grown markedly in recent years.

us meet formally twice a year – once to motivate for our personal choices, and once to give feedback on how funds were deployed and what we have learned. The impetus and desire to help others deepens and giving becomes a personal joy.

So far my examples and stories have mostly dealt with specific situations. What I have come to understand, however, is that making a difference is particularly powerful in the context of the everyday.

From a business perspective, how does the company conduct itself day in and day out? What happens when no-one is looking? Is the culture such that each day, every day, employees act with integrity, bringing the organisation's values to life? Do they look out for others, and seek always to act in the customer's best interests?

From a personal perspective, how do we live our lives? Are we intolerant of difference, insensitive to the pain of others, selfish in the pursuit of our own goals and quick to judge? Or do we bring a kinder, more generous-spirited way of living and engaging with the people around us?

When I was CEO of St.George, a customer gave me a small card inscribed with these words:

> Let there be kindness in your face,
> in your eyes, in your smile,
> in the warmth of your greeting.

The words were Mother Teresa's. I took that little card and put it on my desk in my office where I could see it each day. It then accompanied me to my Westpac office, and is now at home as a steady reminder of how I want to live my life.

I have found that even the smallest things can make a difference: warmly greeting receptionists and security staff as you walk into the building, engaging with people in the lift, acknowledging others by stopping to say hello, putting a smile in your eyes and in your voice, writing a quick thank-you note for a job well done, and giving a team member a hug, perhaps for no reason at all. I have also found that the more these everyday small human connections – in the office, in the community and at home – become just normal things to do, the happier and more fulfilling life becomes.

Let me conclude this chapter by returning to the beginning. The business of business is not just business. Businesses exist to serve society, and have responsibilities to a broad range of stakeholder groups. We are living in a world of increasing income disparity and growing anger and distrust towards institutions. The benefits that globalisation has brought have been unequally shared. In addition, the advent of artificial intelligence, machine learning, robotics, cloud computing and end-to-end digitalisation of processes means that existing jobs are being displaced and new skill sets are urgently required. Businesses, particularly big businesses, cannot simply and without warning lay people off on the basis that their jobs no longer exist and that their skill sets are dated. They have a responsibility to do more. Actions to take include the building of a continuous learning culture, targeted reskilling programs that are attractive and easy for existing employees to undertake, as well as designing jobs differently and more flexibly. It is essential to anticipate change, and to provide employees time and genuine help in transitioning. As for incentive remuneration for senior executives, current models are still too weighted to short-term outcomes. This needs to change. It is long-term sustainable performance that matters.

This is an exciting time to be in business. And there has never been a greater need for businesses to step up and deliver for all their stakeholders. Making a difference is powerful. It is a force multiplier.

5

TRANSITIONING TO
A NEW PHASE

On 28 January 2015, I stepped off the plane at Brisbane Airport. I was on my way to say thank you and goodbye to the Queensland team. A fellow traveller walked up the air bridge with me and asked what I was planning to do in a few weeks' time, once I was no longer the CEO of Westpac.

'I can imagine you will suffer from relevance deprivation,' he said.

'No, no,' I immediately answered with a smile. 'Relevance

deprivation is something men are more likely to experience. I think I will be fine.'

Although I knew that leaving my 35-year career in banking – including 13 years as a CEO – would involve a significant adjustment, I really did feel confident that I would be fine and would transition well. There are several reasons for this.

Firstly, stepping down from the position of CEO of the Westpac Group had been well planned, and was on my own timetable. This was important to me, and I am on record throughout my CEO career of saying that I did not want to overstay my welcome and be in the position of having the board tap me on the shoulder and say, 'It's time to go.' Again, this was a lesson from my father. He retired from his lawn-bowls career when it was at its peak. He told my brother and me that it was important to 'hang up your boots' when you feel strong and in control of your own destiny. It seemed to me that seven full years as CEO of Westpac, coming after six years as CEO of St.George, was about right.

In addition, two further essential requirements were met: the bank was in a strong position strategically and operationally, and the board had outstanding internal successors from whom to select. Probably the single most important factor in achieving this serendipity of timing was the quality of the relationship between me and my chairman, Lindsay Maxsted. Trust and mutual respect were high and we worked together on common objectives. As we discussed and planned for the future, nothing with regard to my own situation needed to be written down. When it came, the announcement of my retirement and Brian Hartzer's appointment had all the hallmarks of good preparation and execution. Leveraging its 197-year history, the bank was about to step up to the next stage of its journey with a fresh and innovative new leader. The day of the announcement, 13 November 2014, was a proud day for me.

The second reason I was confident that I would transition well is that I knew I had a lot more to do. While I was not clear on all the elements of my future agenda, I had energy in abundance and was looking forward to shaping this next stage. For a start, certain existing roles would carry through, including my membership of the Group of Thirty, my position as a global adviser to the US Council on Foreign Relations, and being CARE Australia's ambassador for women's empowerment. These are special organisations with amazing people, providing me with opportunities to learn and to make a difference. I was delighted to have more time to devote to them.

The third reason for feeling good rather than anxious about my pending transition was family. Being able to enjoy rich time with the people in my life whom I love most dearly is cause for great pleasure. Our four children, all young adults, are each on their own path in life, carrying with them strong bonds and love for family. No grandchildren yet, but that's certainly something to look forward to.

And what of Allan, my partner in life? Retirement for him is not yet on the agenda, but more time together is. Our immediate priority in starting out in this new life was undertaking a journey back to our African roots. We spent three and a half months in South Africa, Zimbabwe, Zambia and Botswana, and, after attending the June 2015 G30 meeting in Rio de Janeiro, a final week in the stunning wetlands of the Pantanal. Taking time out like this – concentrated time away from mobile phones, televisions and world news – was something we had never done before, and we loved it. Really, really loved it.

We have a lasting record of it, too. Apart from being an excellent paediatrician, Allan is also a writer and poet. Our intensely personal trip is beautifully captured in three bound volumes containing 100 000-plus words, 313 photographs and 137 poems. A special poem for me was one that Allan wrote when we were on Lake Kariba. We had in previous days visited the Kariba Dam Wall, which was built around the time we were born. We had reflected on its immense presence in the gorge, standing in the way of the Zambezi River and controlling its flow downstream. Now we were on the lake itself, temporary residents of Bumi Hills, returning home on a speedboat from a trip up the Umi River. Here is Allan's poem. It is called 'My Beacon'.

I am speeding over Kariba,
With the wind in my hair,
And a song,
For the wall that has stood,
All the years of my life,
So solid and silent and strong.

And I think of the distance
I've travelled,
Since my birth,
Just to get to this place,
It's hard now to tell,
If I journeyed it well,
Or achieved my potential
With grace.

With the sky so immense
High above me,

And the water like glass
Down below,
The darkness has swallowed
The distance,
It's like flying through space as we go.

My companions are silent
Around me,
And the engines are roaring behind,
Are they thinking, like me,
Of the years of their lives,
Are they happy
With all that they find?

There's a beacon ahead
On the mountain,
As we speed with our thoughts
All alone.
Do they each have a light
That guides them like me,
And a purpose directing them home?

I have not been that wall,
All the years of my life,
I have faltered more times
Than a few,
But I've stood as I could,
With the love of my life
And my beacon has always been you.

On our return to Australia, I turned my attention to what else I might do. Three simple criteria guided my decision-making:

1. Is this an industry/business/endeavour that I love, that I really care about?
2. Can I make a difference?
3. Will I keep learning and growing?

Although I was not particularly keen to go down the non-executive-director route, joining the Woolworths Holdings South Africa board ticked all the boxes for me. When I lived in South Africa, Woolworths, with its well-deserved reputation for quality, was my favourite store. Retail is a sector I love. I am deeply interested in the profound changes occurring as consumers shift their shopping patterns and as new technologies and competitors emerge. Reconnecting to a South African business after nearly 20 years out of the country is something I am delighted and privileged to do. Woolworths is an exceptional company with excellent values and sustainability credentials. Its ownership of David Jones and the Country Road Group brings a strong Australian connection, earnings diversification and a growth path. The company has terrific people. It was immediately apparent that there was lots for me to learn and plenty of opportunity to assist. My three criteria were easily met.

Formally reconnecting to education was also a simple decision for me. Teaching was my first love, and it has never left me. My colleagues at St.George and Westpac would confirm that the 'teacher' was strong in me, even to the point of having the CEO draw attention to grammar, spelling and sentence structure in their reports.

Throughout my career, I have prioritised requests to deliver talks and conduct workshops at schools and universities, and have done so in Australia, South Africa, England and the US. To be formally appointed as an adjunct professor at the University of New South Wales is a great privilege and provides an opportunity for me both to teach and to learn. What fun!

One of the things I particularly appreciate in my life after Westpac is having more time and capacity to involve myself in wonderful projects. One example is Project Uplift, an initiative developed by Mike Baird, the former premier of New South Wales. Mike has long had a personal passion for supporting the activities of youth services organisations, including Youth Off The Streets, Southern Youth and Family Services Wollongong, and the Clontarf Foundation. Through Project Uplift, he decided to take this support one step further by developing a program involving eight young people aged 18 to 22 from disadvantaged backgrounds, and eight business and societal leaders serving as the young people's mentors. These 16 people, including himself, would set off on a week-long 'trek' in a beautiful part of Australia for an intense period of connection, togetherness and sharing. The first trek took place in September 2014 in the Red Centre as we tackled sections of the rather arduous 100-kilometre Larapinta Trail. I found it significantly more exhausting than I had anticipated, as well as much more enriching. Our second trek, with a new group of young people, took place two years later in the Top End, in the beautiful Kakadu National Park.

Something amazing happens on these trips. As the days progress and we get to know each other, real sharing occurs. In one-on-one conversations while walking, in small groups having lunch, or all together around the campfire, stories are told and themes of courage, forgiveness, trust, self-belief, choices and resilience are discussed. Each of us learns something important about ourselves, and we grow in our understanding of others. We learn just a little how to walk in one another's shoes.

I came away from each trip with a much clearer perspective and insight into the challenges and difficulties facing many young people in Australia. I was humbled by the determination and inner strength of our young trekkers despite the cards they had been dealt. Their care for each other, inherent compassion and desire to make a difference and follow their dreams were special to witness. I recognised afresh how very fortunate I have been throughout my life, having had loving parents and a safe home, an excellent education, good health and an abundance of opportunity. There is a saying, 'To whom much is given, much is expected'. That saying applies to me.

The first phase of transitioning from my 35-year banking career is complete. The exit from my CEO position has been achieved, I have refreshed myself, and I have taken time and care to set up a well-rounded portfolio with a mix of interests for the future. The next phase of transition now begins. If I am to follow the course of my mother, I have more than a third of my life yet to live. I have no doubt that I will have occasion again to dig deep and take my courage in my hands, and that I will have to draw on my positive attitude to life and rely upon my resilience in this changing world. I will make mistakes and acquire new learning.

My hope, however, is that I am able to use my experience, and the insights and perspectives I have gained over time, to help others. Making a difference is what I aim to do. I hope I can achieve that.

References

PART I: FOUNDATIONS

1. A Lucky Start
Pretoria newspaper quote: clipping in the author's possession.

2. Learning to Learn
[no references]

3. Choose to be Positive
Oprah Winfrey, *What I Know For Sure* (Pan Macmillan, 2014).

4. Love What You Do
'The Horses of the Camargue': poem by South African writer Roy
    Campbell (1901–57).

5. Be Bold, Dig Deep, Back Yourself
Sheryl Sandberg, *Lean In: Women, Work, and the Will to Lead* (Random
    House Group, 2013).

PART II: LEADERSHIP

1. Right People, Right Roles
Jim Collins, *Good to Great: Why Some Companies Make the Leap and
    Others Don't* (HarperCollins, 2001), p. 13. Copyright © 2001.
    Reprinted by permission of Curtis Brown, Ltd.
Westpac media release, 20 November 2008, 'Westpac announces
    executive team to lead merged group'.

Andrew Fleming, email to Gail Kelly (Sydney, 13 November 2014). Reprinted by permission of Andrew Fleming.

2. Purpose, Meaning, and the Management of Culture
Group of Thirty, *Banking Conduct and Culture: A Call for Sustained and Comprehensive Reform* (Washington, July 2015).

3. Passion for Customers
Gail Kelly, email to all Westpac staff (Sydney, 1 February 2008).
Westpac Group, *Investor Discussion Pack* (Sydney, November 2009 and November 2015), merger and transformation update (Sydney, December 2009), and employee engagement surveys.
Willis Towers Watson, *Global Pension Assets Study 2016* (London, 2016), p. 12.
Deloitte, *Dynamics of the Australian Superannuation System – The Next 20 Years: 2015–2035* (Melbourne, 2015), p. 2.

4. Lead with Courage
Virgil, *Aeneid*, Book X, line 284 – a phrase shouted by Turnus as he begins the charge against the Trojans.
Westpac Group, *Investor Discussion Pack* (Sydney, October 2008, November 2012 and November 2015).
Danny John, 'Banks agree on a mega-merger', *Sydney Morning Herald*, 13 May 2008.
Westpac merger briefing presentation (Sydney, December 2008), p. 11.
Westpac open letter to customers: Copyright © 2008. Reprinted by permission of Westpac Group.
Westpac Group media release, 10 March 2011, 'Bank of Melbourne to launch in August 2011'. Reprinted by permission of Westpac Group.

5. Deliver Results
Lewis Carroll, *Through the Looking-Glass, and What Alice Found There* (originally published by MacMillan, 1871).
Westpac Group, *Investor Discussion Pack* (Sydney, November 2014), p. 66.
McKinsey & Co, 'Decoding leadership: what really matters', *McKinsey Quarterly*, January 2015.

6. Generosity of Spirit

Gail Kelly, *MBA Research Report: Chief Executive Officer Success and the Development of High Potential Employees* (Johannesburg, 1986).

Nelson Mandela, *Long Walk to Freedom* (Little, Brown, 1994), p. 680, 751. Copyright © 1994, 1995 by Nelson Rolihlahla Mandela. Reprinted by permission of Little, Brown Book Group Limited.

Desmond Tutu, *God Has a Dream: A Vision of Hope for Our Time* (Doubleday, 2004). Copyright © 2004 by Desmond Mpilo Tutu. All rights reserved. Essay 'Truth and Reconciliation' available from http://greatergood.berkeley.edu/article/item/truth_and_reconciliation.

Westpac Group, *Executive Team Charter*. Reprinted by permission of Westpac Group.

7. Diversity is Strength

Westpac archives letter: June 1936. Reprinted by permission of Westpac Group.

Erica Packer, 'Women bank tellers not likely here', *Brisbane Telegraph*, 12 October 1961.

Westpac Group, *200: The Story of Us* (published by Westpac Banking Corporation, 2017).

Equal Opportunity for Women in the Workplace Agency, *EOWA Australian Census of Women in Leadership* (Sydney, 2008), p. 3.

Westpac Group, *Annual Review and Sustainability Report* (Sydney, November 2013) and *Sustainability Performance Report* (Sydney, November 2016).

8. Good with Change

[no references]

9. Resilience

[no references]

10. Engaging with the Media

Eric Johnston and Brendan Swift, 'St.George's Kelly to take reins at Westpac', *Australian Financial Review*, 17 August 2007, p. 1.

Scott Murdoch and Sid Maher, 'Westpac chief Gail Kelly joins carbon tax revolt', *The Australian*, 5 May 2011, p. 1.

Eric Johnston, 'Get off Gillard's back, urges Westpac chief', *Sydney Morning Herald*, 8 May 2012, p.1.

PART III: LIVE A WHOLE LIFE

1. Family – The Most Important Thing
[no references]

2. Being in the Moment
Roger Hargreaves, *Little Miss Somersault* (originally published in 1970).

3. A Woman in Business
Kahlil Gibran, *The Prophet* (originally published by Alfred A. Knopf, 1923).

Malcolm Gladwell, *Outliers: The Story of Success* (Little, Brown, 2008).

Peter Gosnell, 'Banking uber babe invests in Wran', *Daily Telegraph*, 12 August 2006.

World Bank Group, *Women, Business and the Law 2016: Getting to Equal* (Washington, 2015), p. 2.

4. Making a Difference
Milton Friedman, 'The Social Responsibility of Business is to Increase its Profits', *The New York Times Magazine*, 13 September 1970.

Westpac Group, *Annual Review and Sustainability Report* (Sydney, 2009), p. 11. Reprinted by permission of Westpac Group.

5. Transitioning to a New Phase
[no references]

Acknowledgements
Anne Lamott, *Bird by Bird: Some Instructions on Writing and Life* (Anchor Books, 1994).

Acknowledgements

It was about six months after I retired from my CEO role at Westpac that I decided to write this book. I felt both excited and daunted by the project. Public speaking is something that I have done a lot of, but putting my ideas down in a coherent and accessible way to produce a book is not. I decided to start by reading about writing.

My first acknowledgement must therefore go to Anne Lamott, the accomplished author of the beautiful, funny and wise book *Bird by Bird*. I learned from her that writing is hard work and that words don't just flow. I learned that you need to show up and keep showing up despite the terrible early drafts. That you must write about what is true for you, write it clearly and commit to finishing. Thank you, Anne. When I became despondent, I reached for your book to make me smile again.

To get going, I needed advice and support. A big thank you to Mike Bowan, long-time friend and colleague, who shepherded me through the various steps that resulted in my book contract with Penguin. To Hilary Linstead and to the team at Gilbert + Tobin, I appreciated and valued your counsel.

As I progressed, painfully at first, in the writing process, I leaned on family members and friends for help. To my very dear brother and sister-in-law, Trevor and Janet, I loved our conversations over dinner and a glass of wine about the family and our roots. Allan, you encouraged me to put one foot in front of the other, and on our many long bushwalks ensured that I sharpened my thinking. Sharon, my very precious first child, not only did you bring me your wholehearted support and encouragement, but you put your skills as a secondary-school English teacher to work in helping me think through structure and approach. Thank you to a range of friends and colleagues who were kind enough to read early drafts and provide helpful comments and suggestions – Carolyn McCann and Mike Bowan (both of whom read it more than once!), Peter Hanlon, John Arthur, Jon Nicholson, Mike Leeming, John Colonnelli and Tim Ford. Thank you, too, to Phil Coffey, Rob Whitfield, Christine Parker, Scott Tanner, Dhiren Kulkarni, Dave Curran, Rebecca Lim and Matthew Grounds for words of encouragement along the way. I appreciated your clarity on key issues, and the filling in of gaps. I also learned that the same event can generate different memories and emotions!

I would also like to acknowledge Westpac and its 2017 team for so generously assisting me in my requests for reference material, fact-checking and for photographs. This is an extraordinary organisation with very special people in it.

To my publishers at Penguin, thank you for backing me and believing in this book before a word was written. Ben Ball and Rachel Scully, you were both superstars, providing a healthy mix of encouragement and constructive criticism. With Ben and Rachel, of course, comes a team of highly competent and experienced professionals – Anyez Lindop, Katie Purvis, Bethany Patch, Alex Ross and many others behind the scenes. It means a lot to me that you cared about my project.

The most important thank you in the production of this book goes to my extraordinary assistant, Ron Pok, who came with me on the journey to an unknown future when I retired from Westpac. Ron has toiled in the trenches with me and, quite frankly, has been indispensible. It has fallen to him to make sense of my scribblings, written mostly by hand and in pencil. In addition, over the period he has become an expert on all that is required from a writer in the arcane world of publishing. Together we have got through it all and I sincerely thank you, Ron.

I am sure it is no surprise that I have dedicated this book to Allan and to our four children. The constancy of your love and your support for me is the most precious of gifts. I am deeply grateful to each of you.